THE VIEW FROM GOOSE RIDGE

THE VIEW FROM GOOSE RIDGE

WATCHING NATURE, SEEING LIFE

CHERYL BOSTROM

THOMAS NELSON PUBLISHERS®
Nashville

Published in Nashville, Tennessee, by Thomas Nelson, Inc.

Unless otherwise noted, Scripture quotations are from the HOLY BIBLE: NEW INTERNATIONAL VERSION®. Copyright © 1973, 1978, 1984 by International Bible Society. Used by permission of Zondervan Publishing House. All rights reserved.

Scripture quotations noted The Message are from The Message: The New Testament in Contemporary English. Copyright © 1993 by Eugene H. Peterson.

Scripture quotations noted NLT are from the HOLY BIBLE, New Living Translation, copyright © 1996. Used by permission of Tyndale House Publishers, Inc., Wheaton, Illinois 60189. All rights reserved.

Scripture quotations noted NKJV are from THE NEW KING JAMES VERSION. Copyright © 1979, 1980, 1982, 1990 Thomas Nelson, Inc., Publishers.

Library of Congress Cataloging-in-Publication Data

Bostrom, Cheryl.
    The view from Goose Ridge : watching nature, seeing life / Cheryl Bostrom.
    p. cm.
    ISBN 0-7852-6655-0 (pbk.)
    1. Nature—Religious aspects—Christianity—Meditations. I. Title.
BT695.5 B67 2001
242—dc21   00–069529

Printed in the United States of America
1 2 3 4 5 6 PHX 05 04 03 02 01

To Blake, Andrew, and Avery—
gifts from God, all of 'em

Contents

Contents

ACKNOWLEDGMENTS

Every time I turned around, someone helped me with this book. Of course I thank my friend Chris Buri. Not only did he invite me to write for Women of Faith, but he also first envisioned this project—and shepherded my work into the hands of Ray Capp, who found a home for it at Thomas Nelson Publishers. Because of Chris, I had the joy of working with Janet Thoma, whose expertise and enthusiasm taught and inspired me. Anne Trudel, who daily sits as the eye in a hurricane of manuscripts, blew peace into every correspondence and phone call. Lynn Green edited my writing with direct, yet gentle, discretion.

Mona Stuart, Cindy Louws, Cheryl Mitchell, Laura Brisbane, Johanne Roorda, Jan Soto, Connie Kooi, Brenda Roosma, Donna and Jacob Steiger, Mike McKenzie, Donna VanderGriend, Ken Koeman, Ron Polinder, Ruth Posthuma . . .

I could write pages about what each one has meant to me. They have offered excellent suggestions and loving support. All have served me generous dollops of time from kettles already feeding multiple obligations. And they have prayed.

I also thank my grandmother, Imogene Tozier, for watching creation with praise on her lips; my mother, Grey Pohl, for encouraging me to write; and my mom-in-law, Carol Bostrom, for listening. I thank my incredible husband, Blake, who reads every line, offering impetus, balance, and necessary veto. And I will be forever grateful to my kids—Andrew and Avery—who, by their honesty, keep me broken and growing.

INTRODUCTION

FROM THE TOP OF GOOSE RIDGE, WE CAN SEE SPRINGTIME all at once. That's what first drew us here. On one of those May mornings when God opens the taps and floods the land with greenery, sunlight, birdsong, and the smell of willows breaking bud, Blake and I stood on a knoll that lumps up from this rolling bench and breathed in the birth of the season. When the VanDalens, who had cleared and farmed this land, offered to sell it to us, we didn't hesitate.

We built our house on that knoll, and though it's just a house, it does mimic a restful old shade tree. We feel like we are outdoors even when we sit on the sofa. Every window pulls our eyes outside—and the view . . . well, maybe I should tell you about it. After all, most of the essays in this book take place right outside these windows.

When I look to the north, I see the horse barn, garden, and

native trees nestle into rolling pasture. Swallows swoop into the barn, where hatchlings wait in mud nests under the rafters. My grazing Saddlebred raises his head and whinnies as I stand in the window. Am I coming out with apples? Goat thinks so and trots under the electric wire toward me. Behind the animals, a rough-cut fir fence encloses my riding arena. A hundred yards more, and Jake's Pond teems with waterfowl, including the giant Canadian honkers that dominate the sky each fall. From the pond's shores, pasture and mixed forest reach toward the Canadian border, abutting Sauter's land a mile farther north.

West windows open onto more woodlands, a weathered old barn, and our lane, which intercepts the county road and leads to our mailbox. Today our cows graze in the field north of the lane, down which a white pickup is bringing our son and daughter home from school. In June, the sun flames itself to sleep directly between two giant firs standing sentinel in the hilly pasture. The undulating land behind them rolls all the way to the bay.

If I move to a south-facing window, I see the blue-tinged outline of the San Juan Islands, twenty-some miles distant. Lummi Island rises from the water like a snoozing dog; Orcas Island peeks over its backside. Our ridge flattens out to the south, joining the wide valley for its run to the sea. Another goose-filled pond, a field full of Hereford bulls, old gambrel-roofed barns, and assorted farmhouses dot the landscape.

Pastures wrap them all. In our south field (near the orchard), Molly is hunting voles—the fat, slow-moving rodents that the aged cat still deposits regularly at the back door.

I like the view from the east windows best. As I look through them, the dogs are lying in the shade. A younger cat, Droopy, scratches the glass door to come in. Where our lawn ends, pasture runs the rest of the way down the hill to where it meets the creek, two more ponds, and—off the house's northwest corner—an old forest, tangled with underbrush. A year-round spring fills the ponds and waters the fir, cedar, maple, wild cherry, birch, and alder trees that grow there. South and east of the woods, forty-acre sections of grassland string through the valley. Fencerows divide them, and silos rise like mileposts from the dairies that claim them. Postmas, Steensmas, Siebrings, and Smits farm there—good neighbors all.

Twenty miles east, past our town, creeks, fields, farms, rivers, and forests, the foothills of the Cascade Mountains rise abruptly, their smooth contours in sharp contrast to the jagged peaks—Church, Shuksan, Baker, Sisters—that bite the sky behind them. Month after month, I get up early to watch the sun march the length of that range, rising explosively at a different spot each day while the earth tilts with the seasons.

I don't like to miss the sunrise at Goose Ridge. It's a powerful reminder to me of Zechariah's prayer in Luke 1. In it, he speaks of "the tender mercy of our God, by which the rising sun will come to us from heaven to shine on those living in darkness and in the shadow of death, to guide our feet into the path of peace" (Luke 1:78–79).

That's the Sunrise that has changed my life, the promise that means everything to me. God offered me Jesus, who died so that He could rise and shine away my blackest hours, my darkest self. He can do the same for you.

Tender mercy. Light from heaven. Pathway to peace. God shows them to us daily, repeatedly—and not just in a sunrise, and not just at Goose Ridge. Nonetheless, I pray that as you read these pages, you will spot Him loving you and working on your behalf in new ways, ways you may have never considered before. He delivers His truth through the most unexpected carriers. Spiders. Ponds. Fertilizer. Chickens.

I simply ask you to watch long and listen closely. Through His creation, God speaks.

Cheryl Bostrom
September 2000

Boundaries

Practical fences rim the perimeter of Goose Ridge. Smallish critters pass under them handily; deer leap them at will. We have no need to interfere with *their* routines. Those fences were built to contain our livestock, and they do it effectively. Barring a stampede, we rest in confidence that our horse and cattle will stay within the boundaries of our land.

I wish the interior restraints on our property were as well constructed. While our perimeter fencing is permanent, we haven't finished the fences around our yard or the ones enclosing woods and pond. Until we do, we are using temporary stakes and a single-strand electric fence to reroute the trampling, browsing beasts.

That setup doesn't always work. After all, we are stringing a scrawny synthetic line laced with a few threads of current-conducting metal. It's not very strong. When a 1500-pound animal lunges against it, it only stretches momentarily before it snaps. Trust me; I've seen it happen a few times. The whole scene leaves me crabby.

Last Tuesday a cow had her head under the wire, reaching for grass just outside the fence line. Some phantom fly bit her, and she swung her head up and sideways, catching the line with the back of her neck. Of course its current shocked her, and she jumped, breaking the line as if it were cotton kite string. Before I could groan, we had eight heifers on our lawn.

I was home alone. "This could be difficult," I mumbled to the cat, before I sprinted outside to disconnect the fence charger. I had to tie the broken ends together. A jolt would not brighten my mood.

By now cows were sniffing our lawn mower, sticking their heads in the open garage, tasting petunias. Pooping on the patio.

I was ready to move to town.

"What we need around here," I growled to the nearest fly-covered heifer, "are boundaries that mean something." She blinked and stuck her tongue in her nostril, as cows often do.

When Blake got home, I gave him a play-by-play of the rodeo. (I did get them corralled eventually.) He finally got me laughing about the whole mess, and we changed the subject. Sort of. We talked about the upcoming holidays—and family gatherings.

Ever notice how, when families get together, interactions may break or damage emotional fences? We can accidentally stumble or intentionally lunge through the weak spots in each other's boundaries. We can end up nosing around where we shouldn't, stomping feelings along the way. Serious fence tramplers control, manipulate, or enmesh their way past our "no trespassing" signs. They leave a trail of damage—like cows on the lawn.

Sometimes we contribute to our own fence failures. Our fears—of displeasing people, of anger, of rejection—can weaken our boundaries, allowing folks to walk all over our hearts. When we refuse to be honest about what is truly important to us, we don't show them the fence line.

The Lord speaks strongly about boundary violations. His Word tells us, "Do not move an ancient boundary stone or encroach on the fields of the fatherless, for their Defender is strong; he will take up their case against you" (Proverbs 23:10–11). More than land is at stake here; God cares about both physical and mental territory, and wants us to respect our own and others'. It's the loving thing to do.

Clearly, the Lord likes boundaries. He shows them to us throughout creation. "It was you who set all the boundaries of the earth," wrote the psalmist (Psalm 74:17). Wisdom, speaking in Proverbs 8:27–29, tells us:

> I was there when he set the heavens in place, when he marked out the horizon on the face of the deep, when he established the clouds above and fixed securely the

fountains of the deep, when he gave the sea its boundary so the waters would not overstep his command, and when he marked out the foundations of the earth.

Let's begin to string effective fences—healthy, strong boundaries. We can offer an honest yes or no—can be true to our Lord and to ourselves—even if a loved one disagrees. We can refuse to participate in damaging behavior or talk, even as we can choose positive interactions. God will come to our aid the same way He did for the psalmist, who wrote, "Lord, you have assigned me my portion and my cup; you have made my lot secure. The boundary lines have fallen for me in pleasant places; surely I have a delightful inheritance" (Psalm 16:5–6).

With no hoof marks in the grass.

WINTER CRAWL

LIKE AN OLD DOG, WINTER HAS SCRATCHED THE GROUND, circled three times, then plopped in a heap on our land. Only the occasional pummeling of a frigid northeaster interrupts the season's torrential rains and weeks of broody, charcoal skies. The weather drives me inside, though I go willingly. Limited daylight began slowing me down weeks ago. Now I don't want exercise; I want cookies. By midafternoon the sofa beckons, offering a nap, and I succumb. Phone calls go unanswered, and bookwork piles up—as do laundry, mending, and any of a dozen other chores. Just last summer I would lasso those tasks as soon as they entered my territory.

Unfortunately, my commitments outside don't ebb with the waning light, either. Though Goose Ridge rests in the winter, it doesn't die. Fences blow down, horse blankets need frequent tugs back into place, livestock bellow for hay, troughs empty, stalls need cleaning. Responsibilities cry to me like unattended babies. This time of year I all too often brush them off like a negligent parent.

In earlier years, I fought the annual decline. I would forge ahead, berating myself when my pace faltered in late fall and expecting too much of myself. Besides necessary chores, I would schedule activities suitable for high-energy summer—though meeting those obligations caused me to bark and snarl at those I love best. I simply could not catch up, much less keep up.

First I grumbled at God. "Could there be a mistake here, Father? You know, putting this dismal season and me in the same location? I might have to change how I do things!"

Then I cried for Him to change me. I asked Him to recharge this body that failed me every year. "Lord, jumper cables—*Please!*" No response.

Finally, I surrendered. I'm learning to be thankful for this body that slows with the season. Now, though the hectic music I dance to keeps playing, I sit out a few numbers during these months. Half-finished projects can wait. Should I paint the living room . . . when I can rub my sleepy child's back instead? Not a chance! I almost planned a party for seventy-five guests this Christmas. Tempting, tempting. Then I remembered. I told the encouraging friend, "Naw. Too much work."

I direct my limited energies toward those tasks that sustain life—physical and spiritual. Yes, I feed the stock and clean the barn, but I don't try to work my horse every day. Yes, I cook and clean and teach and love, but I don't sort my files or engineer new projects. I don't even plan to catch up during this season. Instead, I read, think, pray—and go to bed earlier.

I copy gardeners. Orchardists know that to produce sizable apples, they must prune the previous year's branches. Now I prune too; busywork and overcommitments all get thrown on the burn pile. Then I know that when my sluggish sap starts running again, it will produce large, well-formed fruit.

I finally recognize what God has been whispering to me through the driving rain and squishy clay underfoot. In Isaiah 30:15, He says, "In repentance and rest is your salvation, in quietness and trust is your strength."

He wants me to slow down some of the time. He has built a rhythm into all of His creation—including me. Winter is part of life, part of that rhythm. He promises, "I will give you rest. Take my yoke upon you and learn from me, for I am gentle and humble in heart, and you will find rest for your souls" (Matthew 11:28–29).

Later the spring frogs will climb out of our pond singing. Right now they're asleep in the mud.

And that's okay.

GROUNDED

WHEN FLOCKS OF GIANT CANADA GEESE RETURN HERE IN late February, they split up and settle on the ponds dotting our ridge. They honk, patrol, and occasionally roost on our roof peak before they get down to nest-building, egg-laying, and finally rearing their goslings.

But once those babies hatch, the parents rarely honk. Nor do they sail to adjacent fields for leftover corn or tender shoots. Instead, they work discreetly, guarding and caring quietly for their young. Unless some predator threatens, those pairs keep a low profile—by *choice*, or so I thought.

Vernon, our eighty-year-old neighbor, set me straight one day. His family homesteaded just south of us, and he has watched those birds since he was a boy. "They *gotta* stay quiet. Cain't fly, y'know. Won't 'til them goslings take wing." He went on to explain that once the young have hatched, the adult geese molt, losing both flight and tail feathers. They can't fly for up to six weeks, until their babies start testing their own wings. They are grounded.

This amazed me. Why does God make those parents so incredibly vulnerable just when they need to defend and provide for their young?

I asked the same question when our first child arrived. Before he was born, I felt capable, prepared. After all, I had been educated for independence, self-sufficiency. My husband Blake and I had worked hard—earning, building, planning.

Then our baby clipped my wings. All at once I *needed* my husband to make our living, to encourage me, and to cope with my postpartum depression after weeks of baby spit-up and no sleep. My heart melted with love for that soft, demanding little creature, and my own feathers fell off. I was forced to land, forced to need, forced to depend—on my husband, my friends, my family, and my Lord. I, too, was grounded.

I hated it—then loved it. Without independent flight, I learned to turn to God. Years passed, and I practiced trusting Him through indentured labor as a devoted mom. I learned to live more vulnerably. Rather than hiding my failings, I admitted them. Rather than trying to handle problems alone, I confided in others—especially God.

Now my goslings are fifteen and seventeen, and I often spot them running, flapping, and launching themselves skyward for short flights. My own pinions have grown back again, and I, too, can venture farther afield.

But I'll never fly like I did before I was grounded. I want part of me to stay flightless, weak, dependent. Before those days, I never understood what Jesus meant when He said, "My grace is sufficient for you, for my power is made perfect in weakness" (2 Corinthians 12:9).

I molted when our babies were young. Maybe you molted when the scan showed cancer, your husband left, depression struck, or the money ran out. You watched as your flight feathers loosened, blew across the field, and floated down the creek.

Don't hurry to grow them back. You can't anyway, you know. When you reach your limits, when you admit that life is beyond your control and you slump helpless, you can experience another kind of grounding: the deep certainty that God is your "refuge and strength, an ever-present help in trouble" (Psalm 46:1).

In fact, His Word tells us, "Do not let your hands hang limp. The LORD your God is with you, he is mighty to save. He will take great delight in you, he will quiet you with his love, he will rejoice over you with singing" (Zephaniah 3:16–17).

Our Father would have you cultivate your dependency— your flightless grounding—so that you can experience His *groundedness*. But how? Begin by simply slumping toward God—and the greatest safety and peace you'll ever know. When you talk with Him,

⇥ Admit your weaknesses and mistakes.

⇥ Speak your need for forgiveness, rescue, and leadership.

⇥ Ask Jesus to bring you all three.

And He'll have you soaring in His good time.

STROLLING THE SPIT

WE LIVE FIFTEEN MILES INLAND, FAR ENOUGH TO AVOID some of the fog that can hang on the coast, but close enough for a drive to the bay. On a clear day, Washington's San Juan Islands lump up like so many turtles, and like a flat stone, my imagination can skip unencumbered between them as I squint from the rocky shore.

Oh, that feeling of being unencumbered—without *cumber*, or excess baggage. By the time I was thirty-five, I longed to know that freedom as more than my imagination.

Back then, two friends and I drove to the Semiahmoo peninsula after a storm to lunch at a sprawling resort out on its tip. (Earlier generations saw a Native American burial ground and a salmon cannery sit on this skinny spit of land.) Our children were safely stowed with sitters, and we planned to walk that beach before we ate. I was looking forward to a few hours of quiet conversation with good friends—a rare event. In those days, you see, I typically scrambled through my waking hours. Weeks rolled over me like the storm's residual seas crashing on the shore beside me. The flotsam and jetsam of a too-busy life cluttered my house, my time, and my mind. I was tired and distracted.

Funny thing about beach walks, though; they can help change perspective. When I'm walking, I usually look down—for two reasons. First, if I don't, I'll trip on a piece of kelp and fall flat on my face. Second, I find fabulous rocks underfoot, not to mention shells shaped so intricately that they practically shout about their Creator. But when I pause, I look up. Then I scan the swept sky and the curving, washed shore. In that manner I progressed down this beach, alternately looking up and down, taking in the grand and the tiny, the concept and the detail: God's beachscape and the pieces (stones, waves, driftwood, gulls) that make it.

By the time my friends and I came around the south edge of the resort, my scurrying thoughts had calmed some. When I looked up again, I saw an inspiring scene in an unlikely place. Perhaps the beach had prepared me to notice it; who knows? Anyway, we were walking just outside some of the resort's west-facing windows, overlooking the shore and the sea. Inside, sitting in two wing chairs angled toward each other, a man and woman sat, reading hardcover books. Middle-aged, and dressed in sweaters and khakis, they seemed serene, rested, *caught up* on life's tasks, and living that moment together.

Before you read on, close your eyes for a moment and picture it. Feel it! Time tints the memory, of course, so as I think of that scene today, I surely exaggerate my response. I imagine myself stopping in my tracks, mouth agape, and staring at them, marveling.

The Lord stamped that picture into my mind as a picture of simplicity that I did not have—and that He *wanted* me to experience. For some reason, that couple reminded me of the formerly possessed man in Mark 5 after Jesus had cast his demons into those suicidal pigs. Like this pair, he sat there, "dressed and in his right mind." So unencumbered, so uncluttered. Free. Peaceful. And I wanted that.

I don't even remember what I had for lunch that day, but I do know that I began praying for simplicity right then, for God to teach me where and how to yank my life out of our culture's *cumber* and ruckus. I wanted to declutter—my hours, my relationships, my home, and my spirit—and I needed His help. God says yes to prayers like that, and in digestible, bite-sized lessons, He showed me where to begin.

Simplicity. I've learned it's a very good meal.

HUG TEA

AFTER MY DAUGHTER, AVERY, TURNED TWO, MY MOTHER CALLED to say she was sending me the china tea set I had played with as a child. I hadn't seen it for many years, but after I hung up, I did my best to describe it to my kids. When the package arrived a few days later, the children hovered as I unwrapped each piece. Sure enough, familiar roses and forget-me-nots covered the diminutive cups and saucers; gold paint edged their handles.

Four-year-old Andrew immediately wanted me to fill the teapot with water so he could take a swig out of the spout like an army man would drink from a canteen. He also planned to drench the dog, who lay sleeping on a rug under the kitchen table. This time, I hovered, ready to catch the pot if he let go of it. I figured that once I let him swill and splash with it, he would lose interest. He did.

Avery didn't. She started hopping as soon as she saw it, eager to sip from her own teacup as she had seen me do with my friends. Then and there, I spread a dishtowel over a stool, filled the teapot with apple juice, and poured each of us a cupful. We sat on the floor at our tiny table and drank our "tea" together.

We had tea regularly after that. When we wanted to dress "properly," a raid on the dress-up box would yield wide-brimmed straw hats, ruffled gowns, gloves, and pearls—the usual tea party garb. We wore it all.

At age six, she redefined tea parties by taking them outside. She invited me to a camp she had made between two old fir trees—hidden by thimbleberry and wild currant shrubs. She had upended a cardboard box to make a table, then had covered it with plate-sized maple leaves the color of romaine. Our chairs? Smooth stones, each the size of a football. Into that setting she had carted the fragile teacups and set them on the table. Best tea I had ever tasted.

But she didn't stop there. In her seventh summer, Avery wrote invitations to two friends, inviting them and their favorite dolls to an outdoor tea. To prepare, she and I made cookies and muffins and gathered the fixings for a warm, fragrant, peppermint drink. When the girls and their dolls arrived in hats and dresses, we were ready. We had set a small, lace-covered table in the orchard; Avery's canary, whose cage we had hung in the apple tree beside the table, chirped to the wild birds in the surrounding branches. For an hour the girls, with dolls in their laps, enjoyed tea in that magic setting.

In the ensuing years, Avery often would ask if I wanted some tea. It wasn't unusual for us to sit together, sipping and reading. One Saturday morning, she brought me tea and toast in bed, then leaned back on a pillow beside me. We had been talking awhile when I noticed that she had only taken a couple of sips. "Is your tea too hot, Avery?" I asked.

"Oh, no, Mom. It's fine. I just don't like tea that much, you know."

No, I hadn't known. I glanced over at my sparkler of a daughter, who kept on talking, not realizing that she had just thrown a word rock at me. I had to think about this.

Her animated friendliness told me she meant no harm, so I swallowed my surprise with my next sip, and realized that for Avery, the taste *of* tea had nothing to do with her taste *for* tea. She simply enjoyed what tea *meant:* conversation and time spent together. The fact that a warm herb beverage went along with it was inconsequential.

Not too long ago, I was hurrying to get ready for an overnight retreat. (Think about the contradictions in that sentence!) From the other room, Avery called out the familiar question: "Want a cup of tea, Mom?"

"Not just now, honey," I replied. "I'm getting ready to go." I proceeded with my packing.

Within five minutes, she plopped, wilted, onto my bed. "I need a hug," she mumbled, her eyes downcast.

I stopped in my preoccupied tracks. Teatime really was a

hug-time, and I had just turned it down. Whether with delicate china cups or sturdy, hand-warming mugs, during teatime we embraced each other with our words and our hours. In that setting I could show her my love—as well as the love of our Father, who says, "As a mother comforts her child, so will I comfort you" (Isaiah 66:13).

I dropped my hair dryer and curling iron beside my suitcase, sat down beside her, and draped my arm over her shoulder, hugging her close.

"Is peppermint okay?"

Brain Clutter

Our elderly retriever, Rookie, trembles during thunderstorms, then panics and runs. Though her flight is now a stiff-legged hobble, she's gone at the first lightning flash. During last summer's raspberry harvest, she took off during an ear-splitting, afternoon tempest. Not until 11:30 that night did a berry farmer find her wandering his fields—miles from Goose Ridge.

We try to spot those anvil-headed clouds building in the foothills. Then, if we can't keep her with us, we pen her up. That helps us (because we don't spend hours looking for her), but it doesn't help Rookie. Even safe inside her kennel, her anxiety rages until the storm passes; she pants like a woman in labor. In years past she has splintered doors and worn her teeth to nubbins trying to escape. We have returned home to find piles of debris from her frantic digging and chewing. Her anxiety can *really* make a mess.

So can yours and mine. I am convinced that mind clutter—usually some form of anxiety or depression—often causes physical clutter. I realized that connection after I had spent a decade looking for ways to conquer my own cluttered calendar and home.

I used to blame my lack of peace on having too much to do. I either raced through days, or I procrastinated, stuck in mental mud. Both courses left me trailing junk. No, not Rookie's splintered doors or shredded throw rugs, but piles of paperwork, unfinished projects, weedy flowerbeds, and "stuff" scattered throughout the house.

I should have been rooting out the *source* of upheaval: choices I had made that had alienated me from God, and left me fearful, distracted, or hopeless.

As you read this, you may have a mess on every counter, a bed unmade for weeks, and a car full of muffin crumbs, coffee cups, and junk mail. Your vacuum runs on electricity, you think, but it's been a while . . . and you hope passionately that visitors won't need to use the bathroom, because you don't want to resuscitate anyone who risks stepping into yours.

You wonder, *If decluttering my mind is the starting point, how do I begin?*

First, look past your littered home to your untended mind clutter. Avoid making excuses and blaming your physical state on your circumstances. Recognize that the mess in your kitchen, or bedroom, or family room may be an outward sign of your misshapen thoughts.

Next, dig out the Ten Commandments (yes, those dusty edicts from Exodus 20). With that list beside you, do some detective work. Ask our gentle, honest God to reveal how ignoring these guidelines is messing up your living room.

Here's how my own investigation went:

Commandment 1: "You shall have no other gods before me." My eyes popped open here. I saw that I had sought approval from *people* more than from God. That was enough to get any heart racing with fear. Imagine, choosing to please fickle people over our steady, loving Father! Why would I do that? I dug around in my memories and found reasons. I scrutinized them (an important step), then moved on.

Next, Commandment 2: "You shall not make for yourself an idol." This clearly connected with number 1. Sure enough, I had exalted my husband, kids, health, home, and self—rather than my Creator. Instead of thanking and trusting Him to care for them, I clutched them, idolized them, then worried about them excessively.

And so it went. When I hit Commandment 4, "Remember the Sabbath day by keeping it holy," I knew I had ignored God's gift of rest. That alone would throw my body out of whack!

"Honor your father and your mother," Commandment 5. Here, God wanted me to honor a parent who had brought me great pain. I fought this commandment, but finally understood that letting go and trusting God to teach and heal that parent freed me to live in truth. What could bring more honor?

I saw how my tongue murdered (Commandment 6), how I exaggerated and flattered (Commandment 9), and how I longed for a friend's possessions (Commandment 10). Sobering, humbling, yet *freeing*, when I confessed those problems and then let the Lord forgive and change me.

This process took years. Habits like these don't just dissolve. I needed—and still need—God's power to rebuild. He set to work dismantling defenses, hauling off rotten thoughts, remodeling me with His love. Gradually He is, as Paul describes in Romans 12:2, transforming me by renewing my mind—just as He will for you!

And guess what? As a by-product of this mind-sweeping, my house grew tidier, more orderly. Over time, changes in my mind showed up in my home.

Simplicity happened.

HOUSECLEANING

DURING FEBRUARY AT GOOSE RIDGE, A QUIET RIOT OF growth begins. In the woods I scuff the ground beneath a Douglas fir and spot new root fibers reaching like fingers toward unexplored soil. Buds swell in birches, maples, ninebark. Cedars remain secretive for weeks yet, but don't be fooled; they, too, are stretching toward May.

In town, houses hide their occupants. People stay inside. Are they bored? Languishing as they wait for spring? Hardly! Inside, boxes fill with old shoes, mismatched dishes, and trinkets. Sure as May, yard sale season is coming.

Once the rhododendrons bloom, handmade signs go up everywhere: "Five-family yard sale," they announce. You want a bicycle? A playpen? A propane camp stove? You name it, you'll find a poster stapled to a telephone pole pointing you toward the yard sale offering it.

When Janet invited me to join her sale, I borrowed saw-horses and plywood sheets for display tables. Typical enough. But my participation resulted from no ordinary housecleaning. You see, the Lord had been uncluttering my mind for awhile. My home had begun to respond to the peace He was giving me. I was saying good-bye to extra stuff that demanded my time and energy and hello to greater simplicity and order.

To do that, I shook fall's remaining apples out of an old wooden box and fed them to our horse and goat. Then I set that box in a kitchen corner. Though I had planned to put just one item a day into it, I filled it, and several others, fast. With growing confidence, I *passed the stuff on* at Janet's yard sale and elsewhere.

The terminology is significant here. Through His Word, God calls me to be a *steward*—a manager—not an owner. I was *passing things on* for others to use or enjoy, not just throwing them away. Sure, I came across some junk that needed to be discarded, but that was easy. I struggled with surrendering what most folks stockpile: memorabilia and items that I "just might need someday."

Now let's be sensible. I am not asking you to put heirloom jewels in a shoebox to plunk down on that plywood sale table. If you like that jewelry, by all means, keep it. But if you don't, will it really matter to a deceased great-aunt if you sell or donate her gargoyle earrings? Your grandmother's purple celery tray matches nothing in your house and no one else in the family wants it. Have you confused keeping that tray with loving your gentle grandma? Honor her with joy in your simplicity—not by keeping that piece of glass.

When we unnecessarily accumulate, our stuff starts to steal from us—and it makes us poor. We spend so much time tending things from yesterday that we have little energy left for today. Remember the manna—the bread that God gave the Israelites each day as they wandered in the desert. When they tried to store it, maggots riddled it, and it began to stink.

What you and I choose to keep or pass on will differ. But whether our boxes take days or months to fill, we can each ask a few questions to help us decide:

Am I keeping this to avoid emotional pain? I asked myself if keeping Grampa's wheelbarrow kept him close to me. Was I counting on it for comfort instead of trusting God with my memories, my relationships? I took a picture of it, then took a deep breath and let it go.

Am I keeping this to protect me from fear? Why was I keeping all those cookbooks I hadn't opened since before my children were born? Was I afraid that I might need them later? Worried about my future meals? Rather silly. I passed on the books, freed up shelf space, and ditched my fear. Trusting God made a lot more sense than worrying.

Am I keeping this because I think I should? I didn't like the pink and green cross-stitched llama my sister made for me, but I feared hurting her feelings—and so I hung on to it. Faulty thinking, that. I eventually learned to treasure the gesture and the giver without revering the gift itself.

I am still learning. I have passed on some things I wish I hadn't—but I am getting along fine without them. I do know that peace and simplicity taste good, and that God likes them too. That's why I keep filling that apple box in my corner.

MENTORING ANNIE

IN THE LATE '70S, A TWELVE-YEAR-OLD NATIVE AMERICAN girl named Annie sat in my classroom day after day—quiet, expressionless. Whispers from classmates alerted me to her problems: an alcoholic, abusive dad, an absent mother, responsibility for several siblings. As I heard her story, the weight of her world descended on me, and I felt inadequate to help her carry it. Concerned, I befriended her—but she didn't let me get too close.

One day I invited her home for supper with us, and to my surprise, she came. Blake and I didn't have any children yet, so just the three of us sat down to eat together. Nothing fancy. After I took her home that evening, I remember my shoulders sagging with discouragement over my inability to reach her. Our conversations, though friendly, had remained superficial and were punctuated with silence.

In the back of my mind lurked the facts: First, her tribe discouraged non–Native Americans from intervening in the lives of tribal families. Second, she wouldn't open up, so talking with her was difficult. Third, public school restrictions kept teachers from witnessing to students, and I was afraid to try. Consequently, I didn't say much to her about Christ. And so I stumbled along, loving her as best I could.

One evening fourteen years later, our phone rang. Annie's voice came through on the other end. "I just want to thank you," she said quietly. "I'm a Christian now—because of you." I racked my brain. I had never felt free to share the gospel with her. I thought I had failed her—and God—miserably.

"How?" I asked, dumbfounded.

"Remember that night you invited me to your home? Your husband prayed over the meal. You sat with me, and I felt safe. I wanted your peace. I wanted your God."

Now, I don't remember myself as particularly peaceful back then. Rambunctious and high-strung better defined me in my mid-twenties. The Lord's peace was just beginning to seep into my bones, to become part of my makeup. You have to know, too, that my husband prays sincerely, but briefly—and surely not eloquently. I don't remember a word of his dinnertime blessing that day.

Oh well. It was enough. The Lord magnified our feeble attempts to love a hurting girl. Through us, she absorbed His love. She watched and learned. We thought she saw our failure, but she looked past us, and saw Christ instead. He mentored her in spite of us. Though our amateur gestures had offered her mere swatches of His hope, truth, and love, God stitched those pieces together into a warm quilt. Annie eventually let Him wrap it around her.

That's a fabulous fact about walking with Christ. Mentoring takes a different face. We don't need to be successful, just willing. After all, God brings the success. He can take our most halting, fearful efforts and transform them into exactly what another person needs.

These days I draw courage from Jesus' words in Matthew 19:26. He reminds me that "with God all things are possible." Now I pray that whenever I look at a child, I'll remember Jeremiah 29:11: "'For I know the plans I have for you,' declares the LORD, 'plans to prosper you and not to harm you, plans to give you hope and a future.'"

Annie now has four kids of her own. She also works with her tribe as a director of early childhood education. She is helping parents and children—and, most certainly, spreading the love of the Father who met her at our dinner table.

·

The Nest

Newborn puppies sleep in a lump. They crawl on top of each other, and their legs, tails, noses, and bellies all tangle in a twitching mound. Our memories do that too. Years pile up and merge, details forgotten. Sometimes, though, a memory will stay distinct—like the odd pup that sprawls beside the heap of his snoozing littermates.

I have a memory like that. It happened on Washington's Olympic Peninsula, the rugged forest country where I grew up. Logging enjoyed a heyday there in the 1950s, and I saw its evidence daily. Expansive clear-cuts reminded us children of where our fathers got our bread. Logging trucks rumbled and screeched through town, hauling old-growth cedar and fir to the plywood, paper, lumber, and shake mills that rimmed the harbor.

In those postwar days, we didn't give a thought to displaced wildlife or fouled salmon streams. We lived in the land of plenty. If logging took a few trees and fish, what difference did it make? Those rivers and mountains held an endless supply.

Within a year or two after a clear-cut, the forest did indeed start to grow back. Before the replanted firs took off, thimbleberries, alders, and vine maples jumped up. Mule deer browsed and multiplied, well fed on undergrowth that could now see the sun.

Some birds flourished too. Flickers and wrens sought nests in rotting snags left by loggers. Finches built shallow cups amidst salal shrubs. Robins and thrushes constructed sturdy, symmetrical homes in leafy foliage. Bushtits wove hanging, gourdlike pouches for their young.

My mother knew how birds lived, so after the babies had fledged and the parents had flown, she took my younger brother Vincent and me into the new forest to hunt for nests that she could display on our living room bookcase. That's where this particular memory begins.

One October day we parked on an old logging road, pulled on boots and gloves, and then trudged into the brush. We had our tools: pruning shears, a slow pace, and a bit of a squint. Studying the trees paid off. Together we found a perfect robin's nest, woven of twigs and lined with smooth mud. Momma clipped its branch, and then laid the whole assembly in the trunk of the car. "Nice," I commented, "but who gets this nest, Mom? Vince or me?" My brother and I were competing, you see, clear-cutting those nests. Whoever got credit for the most nests won.

Then it happened. Our mother found a most marvelous treasure: a hummingbird nest. Lichen-covered and bound together with spider's silk, its downy cup was no more than an inch and a half across! Only weeks before, it had held bean-sized babies. I imagined their iridescent feathers, the trembling, whirring engines that sustained them, the nectar and gnats that nourished them. I could scarcely breathe.

When Momma took us to the woods that day, little did she imagine how that nest would follow me down the years, how it would change my hearing and eyesight. Though I still gather nests today—and arrange them on my walls and shelves—I long ago quit counting them. That day in the clear-cut, I began to *see* nests. I felt an awe well up inside that God later explained to me in Job 12:7–10.

> But ask the animals, and they will teach you,
> or the birds of the air, and they will tell you;
> or speak to the earth, and it will teach you,
> or let the fish of the sea inform you.
> Which of all these does not know
> that the hand of the LORD has done this?
> In his hand is the life of every creature
> and the breath of all mankind.

Through that hummingbird nest, God mentored me. He taught my breath to catch as alders spring from the floor of a harvested forest, as salmon rest behind stumps lodged in their streams, and as naked baby birds thrive in nests made of cottonwood down, lichen, and spider webs.

Or in common nests made of mud and twigs.

STAKING BARTLETTS

MY HUSBAND BLAKE HURRIED INTO THE KITCHEN. "COSTCO has fruit trees for $7.95. Good ones." I grabbed my coat and followed him to the truck. Planting trees has always scored high on our "Very Favorite Things to Do" list. We've planted dozens of trees at Goose Ridge, from sugar maple and sweet gum to lodgepole pine and grand fir. We had talked for years about building our orchard.

"What varieties?" I asked, as the truck accelerated and headed south.

"Everything," he replied. (I knew that would include cherries.)

"Any apples?"

"Yup."

"Pears?"

"I think so."

A crowd had gathered around pallets holding bags of twigs, but sure enough, vigorous, two-year-old trees were standing there, well-shaped and grafted to rootstock that grows efficiently around here.

I crouched and crawled into the middle of the apples, right between the pollination chart and a talkative toddler, whose parents discussed Gravensteins a few feet away.

Gala, Spartan, Jonagold . . . I grinned. I could already see them blooming, taste their fruit in apple crisp. I snatched the last Gala, inspected the other varieties like a sergeant examining a new recruit, chose two, then scrunched my way to the pears.

By the time I had found a Bartlett and a D'Anjou I liked, Blake had filled the cart with cherry trees. Never mind that birds devour and rain splits cherries around here. Future Julys would find us wobbling on tall ladders, netting our trees against winged marauders. Montmorency, Bing, and Royal Ann would somehow grow at Goose Ridge.

On our drive home, the truck cab became our council room. After all, birds and rain would be the least of our problems. We plotted strategy for our new trees' survival against the high winds they would inevitably face. We couldn't just plant them. We knew we would have to stake them too. For each one, we would pound two poles into the ground on opposite sides of the tree. Then we would string wires through pieces of old garden hose (to protect the bark) and loop them around the tree. Finally, we would attach a wire to each pole a few feet above the ground, allowing some play in the line. Then the tree could bend with the wind, but wouldn't uproot or topple.

Well-meaning folks sometimes stake a tree so tightly that it doesn't move at all. But they don't realize that God designed trees to grow thicker and stronger *because of* the wind. When gusts wiggle it, a tree builds caliper (thickness) at its base and sends down more roots. At first it can only withstand little breezes, but eventually that tree stands firm in a gale.

Rigid staking hinders that growth. When the trunk can't move, the caliper and root system don't develop properly, and the tree stays wobbly, unsteady in a big blow. I once saw a flowering cherry tree staked so tightly that it simply could not flex. Even worse, the bark had begun to grow around the cables holding it in place, deforming the trunk.

Did you know that God raises *us* like well-staked trees? He holds onto us so we don't collapse, but lets us go through hard times, windstorms that ultimately strengthen us. He knows that some kinds of growth come only through pain, and that without pain, we would remain frail, and maybe even emotionally deformed. While shivering in winds of illness, aging, divorce, tough parenting, self-doubt, or even a dear one's death, we can trust Him to hold us steady, even though we bow with the struggle. Because He can overcome it, He *allows* difficulty for the sake of our ultimate good. In

James 1:2–4, God asks us to "consider it pure joy . . . whenever you face trials of many kinds, because you know that the testing of your faith develops perseverance. Perseverance must finish its work so that you may be mature and complete, not lacking anything."

That concept can help us raise our children too. They need the guidance, the staking that our love and discipline offer them. Kids benefit when we give them room to make mistakes and to accept consequences for those errors while they are still sapling size. If they wobble while they are young, and while we parents can keep them from tumbling too far over, they will grow sturdy and wise. If we hold on too tightly, though, afraid to let them feel appropriate discomfort from foolish choices, they will never learn to stand in the wind—to face the moral, emotional, spiritual, and physical challenges that will someday howl around them.

But that's a topic for another day. I've got trees to plant.

WATCHING THE WAKE

MY GRANDFATHER GREW UP IN SOUTHEAST ALASKA, THE third child of early settlers in a little town called Wrangell. His dad, my Great-grandpa Grey, fished, hunted, and ran traplines to support the family. He weaned Grampa Syd and his siblings on tales of that land's abundance. He showed it to them too. They gathered garnets along the Stikine River, dodged bears at Anan Creek, pulled shrimp from Red Bluff Bay, hooked crabs in Murder Cove, and caught salmon everywhere. Beaver, otter, and mink pelts warmed their bodies and their pocketbooks. The children knew where the creatures lived and how to harvest them.

As the years passed, Gramps moved south and into other ventures, but he never lost his fascination and love for that country. Every summer for thirty years, He and Gram navigated the waters from Port Angeles to Glacier Bay in his classic wooden boat, sharing with childlike enthusiasm the wonders and bounty of that land.

Though ocean swells made me squeamish (a grave embarrassment in our seagoing family), I traveled north with them several times. We began each voyage the same way. As we embarked, Gramps would don his weathered old captain's hat, then light a miserable cigar. By the time we would swing into open water, I'd smell like a stogie.

Today that might drive me onto the deck and into fresh air, but not then. I sat for hours with Gramps in that wheelhouse. I watched him check his compass and swivel the huge, old, wooden wheel to keep us on course. He would march the parallel ruler over his charts, then drive the mile marker behind it. He would plot a route for me, then turn the wheel over to me.

I paid attention pretty well in the narrower channels. After all, I had to contend with submerged rocks and tide rips. But in the open expanses, I would pay less attention; I would get to gawking at whales and eagles and islands and sky. Gramps would laugh. "Better check your wake, Cheryl." Slowly I would turn back to look at that foamy trail, blushing even before I saw it. Yep, crooked. We had meandered along while I had been enjoying the scenery.

Gramps would point me back to the compass and remind me that even a few degrees of deviation from my course would land us in a different harbor than the one I hoped to reach.

After he died, Gram gave me Gramps's compass and some navigational tools: the parallel ruler and the mile marker. I spent a long time thinking about his hands and how they had walked his tools across the charts, measuring, planning, figuring. He had been trained well, and so he traveled confidently and courageously over wild lands and waters.

Our days at Goose Ridge bear a striking similarity to those times with Gramps. Here, Blake and I live with a growing family in an aging wooden home. We are sailing a culture of risky waters, and we are trying to teach our kids to navigate before they head north—or east, or south, or west—on their own. We have our chart, God's Word, to guide us. Our Father asks us to check our wakes and to adjust our courses. He tells us to watch Jesus, our Compass, and to teach our kids to do the same, so that we may all rest in safe harbor at nightfall.

The Lord reminds us in Proverbs 2:8 that "he guards the course of the just and protects the way of his faithful ones." In Proverbs 3:6, He tells us, "In all your ways acknowledge him, and he will make your paths straight." In other words, if we keep our eyes on the Compass as we travel through our days, He will keep our wakes straight.

I close with a prayer asking for just that:

> *Father, we are floating in unpredictable waters. Storms blow in, and reefs hide beneath the surface. We need You, Lord. Please help us negotiate through fogs of weariness and*

confusion. Give us strength to buck the tides of darkness flowing against us. Keep the sharp rocks of conflict and pain from piercing our hulls and sinking us. Caulk our seams and give us plenty of fuel to reach shores full of others who need You. And please swab away our sins so that our decks and holds are clean and our footing sure.

We thank You already. In Jesus' name, amen.

To Open a Hoof

MY HORSE WEEDY HAS ALWAYS HAD GOOD FEET—UNTIL recently. A few nights ago he came up from the east pasture early. On an ordinary day, he would still have been grazing, but this evening Weedy was lying down in his paddock, his right front foot extended awkwardly. When I nudged him to stand, he hoisted himself with a groan, but would put no weight on that painful limb. Had he injured his shoulder? Bowed a tendon as he raced across slippery turf? I ran through possibilities in my mind. Blake, my veterinarian husband, hauled my imagination back to reality. "He's got a sole abscess," he stated calmly. "We'll have to open it up."

Sole abscess? A little foot problem was causing that much pain? Couldn't be. "Look, Blake, he's a bit swollen here, don't you think?" I pointed to an area just above his fetlock.

"No, his leg looks fine. He's picked up an infection in that foot, and the pressure is building. That's why he went lame so fast." To make sure, Blake compressed the foot with hoof testers. Weedy winced.

Then it came to me. In the fall, our blacksmith had trimmed and smoothed my horse's chipped summer hooves and had cautioned me about one spot. "Watch that chip. It's deep, and if you get any bugs in there, he'll abscess. Put some iodine on it and keep an eye on it."

He finished trimming and left. I swept up the hoof shards, fed them to my waiting dogs, and promptly forgot his warning. The foot hadn't looked that bad to me. Now, months later, here was my wonderful, strong-footed animal, dead lame.

Out came the hoof-carving tools, and Blake dug into Weedy's sole. After a few minutes, a hairline black crack showed up where a smooth white line should have been. A bit deeper, and it started to ooze. "We've got it," Blake said. He opened a hole for drainage, doused it with an iodine solution, and put the foot in a hoof boot to keep mud out of the hole. "Weedy will be better in no time," he promised. He gave me a schedule for soaking and boot wearing, kissed the top of my head, then returned to the house.

Now, my women friends don't kiss my noggin, but they can dig into my soul. When we talk, they lance abscesses that damage my footing and rob me of courage or compassion, hope or discernment. I need these women to help soak out spiritually crippling bugs, and then to help me walk soundly.

Paul understood that. In Titus 2:4–5, he explained that older women "can train the younger women to love their husbands and children, to be self-controlled and pure, to be busy at home, to be kind, and to be subject to their husbands."

I take that to heart. I regularly seek out my "older" women friends. We walk country roads for miles, sip tea, pick berries, lift weights, or study the Word. We voice our yearnings, frustrations, joys. As I open my heart's "hoof" to them, my hidden attitude abscess drains away, and its pressure (which in earlier days would often erupt on my unsuspecting husband) subsides.

But I have learned to pray for discernment in my relationships for a few important reasons:

Not all older women are good mentors. Just as I have rolled in the loamy soil of a wise, older friend's guidance, I have also bogged down in the muck offered by women with dusty faith.

Chronological age and spiritual age are two different things. An "older" woman may be my age, or even chronologically younger. But she is one whom the Lord has beautifully groomed and matured through her experiences and her time alone with Him.

Soul carving requires permission. I don't want anyone to muscle into my soul with a carving knife and abruptly hack away at my infections. If a friend were to do that and ignore the Holy Spirit's gentle, patient timing, she would leave me, like Weedy, groaning in pain.

Weedy isn't groaning now. The day after his sole was opened, he walked with a only a slight limp. By the day after that, he snorted and charged across the field, his abscess gone.

GUTTER GARDENS

OUR RIDING LAWN MOWER LIVES IN THE SHED OUT BACK. This creaky, aged tractor has traveled places that make the repairman at Lynden Mower cringe. It has leveled remains of blackberry thickets, ventured into swamp-loving tulle grass, and repeatedly circled trees on the far reaches of Goose Ridge, protecting bark from nibbling rodents that hide in thick-bladed clumps. But unless we're using it, we ignore that machine. Chaff and damp clippings collect on the mower's deck, inviting weeds and grass to germinate there, under our feet and atop the devouring blade. Before we know it, we can look down and see a fertile isle, planted by our neglect.

Meanwhile, a brave fescue has sprouted in a meandering crack in our driveway. A desert garden, that. And what about the blackberry seedling growing in the rot crowning our neighbor's fence post? Intentionally planted? Not at all. Some crow lit there momentarily and left the seed, a remnant from his morning feast. Now it stretches root tentacles into decaying wood and is growing just fine, thank you.

Strangest is our gutter garden. When I climbed the ladder yesterday to patch a dripping joint, a tiny fir seedling peeked over the gutter's lip. How it (and the dust feeding it) found a way to our roof, I can only speculate. Dropped from a nesting bird's mouthful? Hauled in on a dry wind?

After seeing that tiny tree, I started watching. I saw surprise gardens everywhere, sown willy-nilly, and growing in the most unlikely places. Violets peered from under the propane tank. A thistle leaped from a starling's soggy nest in a dilapidated mailbox. In an abandoned rubber boot at a neighbor's dairy, something rather scary grew; I didn't even try to identify it.

I guess I've got words growing everywhere too. After all, I've strewn them far and wide. Sure, some flourish in the raised bed of my planned kindnesses; words in rows, carefully planted, lovingly tended and weeded. I'm not so worried about those. But what happened to the words I threw against my daughter the morning I skipped devotions and drove that stewing teenager to school? Did those words spread like mildew, and damage the fabric of her heart?

And I remember some acrid adjectives, deadly as nightshade berries. I used them to describe someone to my husband one night while I washed lettuce for dinner. So what if the person "deserved" them? So what if I spoke them privately in my own home? Maybe they caught on the breeze, blew out the window, and landed in a freshly-spaded planter box across the property line. What if they trailed down the kitchen drain, found their way into the water table, and then sprayed through a garden hose miles away?

I opened the Word to James 3:9–10, where I read, "With the tongue we praise our Lord and Father, and with it we curse men, who have been made in God's likeness. Out of the same mouth come praise and cursing . . . this should not be."

That night after I brushed my teeth, I stuck out my tongue and stared at it in the mirror. That floppy piece of flesh, such a seed sower. I studied it from all angles, and prayed for the seeds it scattered. I asked that my harmful words would shrivel and die. Even more, I prayed that they would never be sown in the first place. Then I asked the Lord to fill the hopper in my head with Word-seeds that would grow wherever they fell, so that even gutter gardens would nourish and bless their finders.

LEATHERJACKETS

YEARS AGO, AN OLD RHODE ISLAND RED HEN AND I WOULD garden together. Long after the kids had lost interest in spotting new sprouts, she would dig nearby. While I yanked moisture-sucking ironweed out of green beans, sorrel and smartweed out of peas, she'd scratch purposefully, spraying dirt behind her with her powerful legs.

That old hen couldn't have cared less about my funny little plants. In fact, they got in her way. Though I liked to think that she enjoyed my company, I really knew that she wanted the insects I uncovered as I weeded. One day, I stopped working and watched her. With her beak a half inch from the soil, she moved slowly through the rows, much like a cat stalking the end of a trailing string. But unlike a cat, she crooned and clucked as she went. She reminded me of my grandmother, humming while she dried dishes. Without a doubt, that hen was enjoying her pursuit much more than I was mine. So I put down my hand hoe, and helped her hunt bugs.

Then the fun began. I picked cabbage loopers off of broccoli and tossed them her way. A cutworm at the base of a cauliflower was a real find. She cocked her head to watch it, then pecked it twice before swallowing it like I would a bite of pie. Best of all, though, were the leatherjackets, the crane fly larvae that hid in the soil, looking like the gelatinous vitamin tablets I buy at the health food store. She came running for them, and if you have ever seen a red hen sprint, you know I was laughing.

Every fall, those leatherjackets metamorphose into crane flies. Then, over the course of a few short weeks, they crawl out of the soil in fields, lawns, and gardens—legions of them. When I was a child, my grandmother called them "gollywhoppers." They look like mosquitoes, only huge and clumsy, trailing legs like gangly adolescents or half-grown puppies. On occasion, my son likes to catch one of these nonstinging, nonbiting bugs and hurl it at his unsuspecting sister. Mid-trajectory, the freed captive takes flight, and my startled daughter shrieks.

I like crane flies. All year long they quiet my nervous stomach by reminding me of God's remarkable, abundant provision. Their eggs hatch in the fall, and throughout the winter those grubs lie in the earth, feeding the gulls that fly in from the bay. Spring's blackbirds and summer's thrushes gobble them too. Then, just about the time the swallows are flocking, readying themselves for autumn's flight south, the crane flies emerge. They climb out of their leathery skins at exactly the right time—fluttering, plump dinners for the migrating birds.

Year round, crane flies remind me of a promise in Philippians 4:19: "And my God will meet all your needs according to his glorious riches in Christ Jesus." Too, they reinforce Jesus' words in Matthew 6:8 when He tells us, "Your Father knows what you need before you ask him." I can trust that God's physical and spiritual nourishment waits for me. I often have to dig for it, but sometimes . . . sometimes it flies right into my face.

"Therefore I tell you, do not worry about your life," the Lord says. "Look at the birds of the air; they do not sow or reap or store away in barns, and yet your heavenly Father feeds them. Are you not much more valuable than they? Who of you by worrying can add a single hour to his life?" (Matthew 6:25–27).

"Yes," I say to myself, "life is jam-packed with leatherjackets, and in my most fortunate hours, crane flies. Why do I worry about anything?"

BARN CATS

FOR WEEKS THE KITTEN RESISTED HER. AT FIRST MY DAUGHTER Avery could only glimpse the scrawny calico deep in the blackberry thicket and hear her mewling for her missing mother (whom we suspected coyotes had eaten). The tiny kitten's fear kept her huddled in the familiar safety of thorny vines. Undaunted, Avery trudged daily to visit the orphan. She left food at the thicket's entrance, then sat quietly at a distance, watching. At first "Callae" wanted nothing to do with my persistent child. Only after Avery left would she nibble the food—while we watched through binoculars.

Day after spring day, Avery waited. Though Callae eyed her warily, she showed no signs of coming into the open. Avery didn't mind; she enjoyed the mystery of this friendship with a feral creature, the probable progeny of the barn cats that thrive around here. And she saw progress. Now

Callae meowed plaintively when she spotted Avery coming toward her.

I wasn't so patient. I had given up long ago, and was mentally shaping the advice I would bestow upon my child; probably something along the lines of, "If she hasn't come to you yet, she probably won't." Hah! Good thing I kept quiet. On a day like any other, Avery scooped up Callae's food and carried it toward the thicket. But unlike any other day, a young calico padded out of the vines and paused, holding her ground until my daughter stood within twenty feet of her. Wisely, Avery set the food down and retreated. Callae crept forward and ate, with Avery just a sack race away.

Trust grew quickly then. Within a few days, Avery crouched within ten feet. By the following week, she stroked the wiry kitten's back. The week after that, Callae knew the joy of having her chin scratched—and she purred her gratitude. Before long, the kitten bounded across the field to meet her provider, who cradled her in her arms.

The rest of the summer blurred by, as summers often do, until one hot September night Callae gave birth to four babies in a box in our utility room. As she nuzzled and fed her newborns, I knew I was watching my history.

I used to be a barn cat, fearful like Callae—only I hid behind the brambles of self-protection, self-sufficiency. Trusting anyone with my deepest feelings was too terrifying, too much like offering myself to coyotes. I wore masks that said, "I can handle it; everything's fine." And so my heart stayed in a thicket, alone and lonely.

But God knew where I was hiding. Year after year, He sat by me. Even when I resembled a defensive feral cat, hiding and hissing, He stashed food for body, mind, and soul in my path. Best of all, He waited until I quit running and let Him love me. Later I read in 2 Peter 3:9, "He is patient with you, not wanting anyone to perish, but everyone to come to repentance."

Life with God was better. I learned to spend time alone with Him, time when I could jump in His lap and let Him scratch under my chin. I learned to purr freely. And I learned that I could come out into the open with Him. He showed me that I could be emotionally honest, and He would keep me safe.

Please don't think I never get scared anymore; I do. Or that I'm perpetually wise and trusting; I'm not. God is gradually changing me, though, and my children have been brought up under His roof. I have seen how "he gathers the lambs in his arms and carries them close to his heart; he gently leads those that have young" (Isaiah 40:11).

I do believe that a mom who knows she is safe and loved raises children differently than a mother who feels afraid and alone. Even Callae's kittens grew differently because they lived in our house instead of in her thorny hideout.

How, then, can we moms help our kids grow like well-loved kittens—and not barn cats? Matthew 6:33 tells us to "seek first his kingdom and his righteousness, and all these things will be given to you as well." Psalm 37:3 says it another way: "Trust in the LORD and do good; dwell in the land and enjoy safe pasture. Delight yourself in the LORD and he will give you the desires of your heart." In other words, if we follow God out of the thicket and put Him deeply, passionately, obediently first, He will protect, feed, teach, provide, heal, encourage, discipline, guide, cheer, support, and even caress us—and our children.

Under the chin, please.

Two Rides

On his ninth birthday, my son, Andrew, invited nine boys over for the day. After hours of baseball, Slip 'N' Slide, Nintendo, hot dogs, nacho cheese Doritos, cake, ice cream, and carrot sticks (to appease my conscience), the frenzy subsided. A couple of boys had to go home, and the rest settled down to watch NFL Blooper videos.

I was stuffing paper plates into an overflowing trash bucket when Jonathan walked purposefully into the kitchen. I straightened up and greeted him. "I'd like to ride your pony," he said, without a "please" or "may I." I looked at him. He stood there, waiting.

"Well, Jon, do you know how to ride?" I asked.

"I do." Silence. He offered no details to flesh out the extent of his equestrian prowess. I knew Jon's family did a lot of sailing, but I could not for the life of me see how tacking across a choppy strait could transfer to riding. He lived in town, and at age nine hadn't had a lot of years to accumulate solo experiences. So I asked him where he learned.

"I read about it."

That did it. He won me over. Many times visiting children had asked to ride our pony in the "can I please, can I please, I love horses" style that I easily refused. I knew that our crafty little Shetland would pitch an inexperienced rider in an instant unless I led the pony around while the child held onto the saddle. And I sometimes chose to do that. But not for Jon. He had real riding in mind. You know, two reins in his hands. Trotting. Cantering.

"Sure, Jon. Let's go." With a backward glance at the recumbent boys in front of the TV (and a quick phone call to Jon's mom), I headed for the barn with Jon in tow. He asked no questions, but quietly watched while I saddled Ladybug. I plopped a helmet on his head, and led both of them to a small pen where the pony couldn't pick up too much speed and the ground was reasonably soft. After giving some basic instructions for the sake of my pony, I asked him if he had any questions or needed any help.

"Nope."

Part of me was miffed that he thought there was so little to it, but another part of me admired the kid. I had to applaud his confidence.

Then I did something I had never done before. I handed

him the reins and walked away. Well, sort of. He thought I left, anyway. I really walked around the barn and watched him secretly.

Jon managed. He climbed on Ladybug from the left side, put his feet in the stirrups, took the reins up evenly, and gave her a nudge with his heels.

She went forward. She didn't buck. He turned her to the right and left like he was riding a bicycle. He kicked her harder and she trotted. I could hear his teeth rattle. Then he brought her back to a walk, jumped off, and called for me.

I popped my head around the side of the barn. "Yes, Jon?"

"Now I'm ready for the big one."

"You mean *Carlos*?" I nodded toward my Appaloosa, sixteen hands tall, grazing in the west field.

"Yeah, him."

Now Carlos was a rare animal. A big, flashy fellow, he had (before retiring at age eighteen) enjoyed a successful career in high-level dressage, a precise riding discipline used to train warhorses. Yet he was amazingly gentle. He reminded me of a huge dog around kids. Stories trailed after him, tales of how he had actually protected children. And at age twenty-five, he had grown kinder still. I could trust him with Jon.

So I brought Carlos into the barn, tacked him up, launched Jon into the saddle, and sent them off at a walk. But when Jon bumped Carlos into a trot, he lost his balance. He bounced once, twice, and then right off the side of the old horse.

Carlos stopped, mortified, I'm sure. Jon pulled himself to his feet, trembling. He was okay, so I quickly hoisted the reluctant boy back into the saddle, just to regain his perspective. Next thing I knew, he was back in front of the TV, watching Bloopers.

Jon had tested his "book knowledge" that day. Even better, he and I had both practiced courage—he by riding, and I by letting him ride. Typically, you see, I cautioned children, protected them from pain, tried to keep them safe. The thought of their getting hurt frightened me.

"But," you protest, "they need instruction and guidance!" Of course they do. We all know that the world holds some real danger for them. But as they get older, I can't always hold the reins. I must discern between legitimate fear for their well-being and fear that is selfishly self-protective. So that day I bit my tongue and let Jon ride, trusting that pain is a good teacher.

When I don't let go, when I try too hard to control outcomes, I may infuse my children with a spirit of fear—which is not from our Father. "God did not give us a spirit of timidity," wrote Paul, "but a spirit of power, of love and of self discipline" (2 Timothy 1:7). Unfortunately, by filling their minds with warnings, but giving them no age-appropriate freedom to learn on their own, I can make them too afraid to test their values, too timid to stand up for what they believe, too frightened to be flexible. Later, they may even try to quiet their fear through risky, painkilling behaviors.

Instead, I will allow them to fall off horses early on—so that later they will be discerning. "Be strong and courageous," God says in Deuteronomy 31:6. "Do not be afraid or terrified . . . for the LORD your God goes with you." I want my kids to ride life like that.

And not just read about it.

ROCK EATERS

"WHY 35 MILES PER HOUR, MOM?" MY DAUGHTER ASKED. "We haven't seen a car since we left home." As we crawled along at the speed limit on the open country road, I knew my detailed defense of highway laws just wouldn't cut it. Fifteen-year-olds open their ears only briefly. Anything longer than ten or twelve words . . . well, forget it.

"For the birds," I replied. As I spoke, a flock of finches flew up from the roadside, where they had been swallowing bits of gravel. "If we drive too fast along here, we'll hit the rock eaters."

She knew what I meant. Back in her grade school days, when she listened longer, I had explained that many birds eat coarse sand or pebbles to help grind the food in their muscular stomachs, or gizzards. While some birds nibble common roadside grit, others have been known to swallow broken glass, coal, shells, gold nuggets, and even (near a mine in Burma) rubies! Apparently they like anything abrasive that can help break down and digest their food.

For me, Scripture acts like good grit in the gizzard of my soul. When I swallow God's Word, I can better digest the experiences I ingest daily. I can dissect them, absorb their nutrients, and eliminate the toxins.

Our kids need that grit too. Throughout their preschool and elementary school years, we did our best to fill our children's spiritual gizzards with Scripture and stories of how God loves us and works in our lives. After all, the Lord wants us to impress His commandments on our children. He says to "talk about them when you sit at home and when you walk along the road, when you lie down and when you get up. Tie them as symbols on your hands and bind them on your foreheads. Write them on the door-frames of your houses and on your gates" (Deuteronomy 6:7–9).

But when our children hit seventh grade, something changed. Well, lots of things changed. Friends. Attitudes. Their teachability. Researchers like Piaget and Kohlberg would probably say they had entered new stages of cognitive and moral development. Whoopee. All I knew was that the way I had taught them in the past didn't work anymore. Our benevolent dictatorship had become obsolete, and it needed to be replaced by coaches who guided instead of nagged, listened more than they talked, and chose flexibility instead of flexed muscles.

Of course, this didn't happen overnight. My husband and I had anticipated the shift, and so had begun phasing out the old guard by late grade school. Nonetheless, the mental gymnastics of early teens flipped us on the mat. I was often frustrated . . . and frightened. Our children needed Christ's grit more now than ever, but acted bored during devotions and uninterested in my wordy instruction. And they told us so. One child pointedly suggested, "Take off your teacher hat, Mom. I just need you to listen. I'll figure it out."

So I said less—and prayed more. I also watched my own life more. I had no choice. When I drove too fast, or criticized, or pouted, or bossed, or procrastinated, they called me on it. There would be no double standards here. What I expected of them, they watched for in me. And I failed repeatedly. Where I had wanted them to see an exemplary mom, they saw, I hope, a humbled one who needs her Savior's grace—a parent who can't get by without Him.

Birds and people both do best if they eat grit frequently. But sometimes they don't get to it. Ice and snow may cover the stones birds hunt. Attitudes may distract teenagers from swallowing Scripture's grinders. But God understands that, and He has provided for them by making grit last. Stones eaten by bobwhite quail in the spring have stayed in their gizzards and continued to pulverize seeds in the fall. And teenagers can still interpret life with rubies eaten when they were kids . . . until they again choose to peck up Wisdom's gems.

Now, that's good grit.

GOAT GLUE

WHEN OUR NEIGHBOR'S 1971 CHEVY PICKUP LOOPED INTO our driveway last October, the goat was looking out the passenger window, ears forward, nose pressed against the glass. During his seven years of life, he'd never left the farm a mile south of us. Nor had he ever left Kelly, the old mare who had died the previous week. Since he was a kid, he had slept in the stall next to hers, grazed beside her, and even stood under her belly to escape summer sun. After her death, he bleated a requiem that jabbed the hearts of all who heard.

Now he was coming to live at Goose Ridge. Because trucks had hauled our cattle to their winter lodgings, my horse, too, was lonely. We humans hoped this new friendship would comfort them both.

At first the goat nervously trailed behind Weedy, baffled by the unfamiliar horse's posturing. Weedy would flatten his ears, then wave his head menacingly to keep the goat at bay. When the goat persevered, Weedy bit him and even struck at him with his front feet. Only thick fur and agility protected the little pygmy from harm.

We fought our impulses to intervene and instead intentionally ignored the goat. If we rescued him, he would be inclined to attach to us instead of Weedy. If that happened, we wouldn't be able to keep him.

Goats, you see, can escape most enclosures. This one was no exception. He hopped right through fences that restrained our larger livestock. He needed a woven fence to contain him, and we had none. If we were to build the goat his own, smaller pen, we would defeat the purpose of our plan. Both horse and goat would be alone again.

Clearly, for this new arrangement to work, Goat needed to bond to Weedy, to *want* to be with him. We hoped he wouldn't require any fences.

Pretty bold thinking, huh? We questioned the wisdom of it a few times ourselves. Within the first week our neighbors called, wondering if we knew anything about the goat on their back lawn. Shortly after that, the kale in my patio flowerpots disappeared. Even when he ripped bark from a cedar sapling in the yard, I remained resolute. I really liked the little guy and believed that if he eventually devoted himself to the horse, temptations elsewhere wouldn't entice him so much.

Sometime during the dark, soggy days of December,

Weedy and Goat did indeed bond. Weedy no longer made menacing swipes at him. Instead, any dog that got too close to Goat would have to contend with the protective horse. More than once I watched Goat run to Weedy and hide behind him until the "danger" passed. Goat now crawled under the gate to sleep in Weedy's stall. And though he could go anywhere he wanted, he stuck with Weedy like glue.

One day I tied Goat behind the barn so that I could clean the stall without the playful critter butting me. Weedy whinnied and Goat bleated until they could again see one another. At last Goat's attachment was sturdier than any fence.

Our son will be eighteen this summer, and you know what? He's a lot like Goat. As a five-year-old, he chopped not my kale, but my lilies—while brandishing a wooden "sword," wielding a garbage can lid, and wearing a red cape. Then somewhere in the dark, foggy years of junior high, a commitment he had made earlier to our Savior took hold—and he began to follow Him. Everywhere.

Now my husband and I don't spend our time thinking about how to build stronger fences to control him. His control is internal and directed by the Holy Spirit. Perfect child? No, but as much as we love him, Jesus loves him more—as He does all His kids. He promises, "I know them, and they follow me. I give them eternal life, and they shall never perish; no one can snatch them out of my hand" (John 10:27–28).

Parenting calluses knees, sure enough. Uncertainties throw

us onto them as we ask the Lord for guidance. We waffled plenty, wondering how to raise our children. But we would do a few things exactly the same if we had it to do over again. Early on, we brought our children to Jesus. We kept tight boundaries around them, and we worked hard to keep their spirits soft and teachable. But as they grew, we first expanded, then pulled down our fences, gradually lifting external controls so that our kids' bonding to God could deepen.

We still pray that once grown, they will follow God gladly, freely—whether we are there or not. And we are trusting that no one can snatch them out of His hand.

No one.

RUNNING WITH CINDY

MY LEGS ACHE. COME TO THINK OF IT, SO DOES THE REST of me. And it's all because of Cindy. She's the one who got me running again. Really running. It happened like this.

Several weeks ago, I crept into the fitness center. I hadn't lifted weights for close to four months. Just as I climbed onto an inner-thigh machine with stirrups like a gynecologist's exam table, in walked Cindy. Bad enough that I didn't even recognize my legs. They had hidden under warm, fuzzy clothing all winter, and apart from cursory rubdowns after showers, I had ignored them. Now here they were in shorts—flabby, pale, and attached to my torso; I had to claim them.

She didn't seem to notice. Instead, she told me that two months before, she had begun distance running for the first time ever. And she liked it. She was so . . . *joyful* about the whole thing. Before I knew it, I had told her about my running days, nearly fifteen years earlier. And then she accomplished what my husband had been unable to do in all that time: she rekindled a spark of enthusiasm in me for the sport. Stranger still, I planned to meet her the following Friday to log a few miles.

I guess I finally wanted to trade negative pain for positive pain. After all, failure to exercise hurts. When I haven't been working out, my body aches, my mind dulls, my stamina wanes, my irritability rises, my self-esteem drops, my motivation disappears, my health declines, and I gain weight. Ouch.

So why do I choose the sofa and a cinnamon roll instead of exercise? Is it easier? No, all that aching, dulling, waning, rising, dropping, disappearing, declining, and gaining is definitely not easy on a person. Does it feel better to eat and loll? Only momentarily. Soon it feels worse! Why, then? The apostle Paul explained it well: "Now if I do what I do not want to do, it is no longer I who do it, but it is sin living in me that does it" (Romans 7:20).

Yep. My problem here is laziness, part of that old sin nature in me. Working out takes . . . well . . . *work!* Who wants that discomfort? Cindy convinced me that *I* do. She reminded me that exercise would benefit every part of me. Once I got moving, the aches and pains from disuse would subside. I would think better, sleep more soundly, heighten my optimism, get sick less, increase my endurance, and shoo away fat. But most significantly (and here she tore me away from my self-centered focus), I would be obeying God's Word, which says, "You are not your own; you were bought at a price. Therefore honor God with your body" (1 Corinthians 6:19–20).

That struck home. All my excuses about not having enough time, or being too tired, or waiting for better weather, sat like rats trapped in a cage, blinking because the lights had been flipped on. They were caught and exposed. And I hauled them out of my house. Too often I had focused on obeying God with my mind and heart—and not with my body. No more.

I want to follow Him completely, with all of me. That means that one way or another, I will move this body He gave me. Out of gratitude to Him—and with His help—I will celebrate running with Cindy.

She and I run regularly now. After a long winter, I am exchanging the pain that my laziness caused for the pain of growth, and improvement, and hope. If my muscles ache a little bit as I get stronger, oh well. They're just grumbling about having to leave the couch.

Let them.

SIMPLE STAMINA

WANT TO HEAR MY "TO-DO" LIST? I IMAGINE IT WOULD sound just like yours: a thousand items long, and yapping loudly. Last week I sat down with that list and tried to organize it into bite sizes. I kept sitting. Then I mapped out an efficient strategy for task completion. Didn't work. I just looked at it and chucked it onto my overflowing desk. Yesterday, though, I made progress. Yesterday, you see, I wrote down a five-step plan for stamina. *I can do that,* I thought.

I pushed back my chair and immediately followed step one: I went to bed early. About time, too. Here in the bright energy of an accelerating spring, I had been pushing myself for weeks. Now I had exhausted my mental reserves. With each new task's demands, I felt like my recalcitrant goat, who plants his little hooves, then gags and chokes while I tug on his collar to lead him where he doesn't want to go. Fatigue will do that. In 1 Kings 19:4, Elijah, afraid and exhausted, said to God, "I have had enough, LORD." He had lost his desire to press on. So what did he do next? "He lay down under the tree and fell asleep" (v. 5). The Lord knew he needed sleep before anything, to replenish his brain chemicals and to allow his body to recuperate. I needed that too. So, like Elijah, I slept.

By the next morning, I could face step two. I drank water—several glasses throughout the day. In my sleep-deprived state, I had been drinking too much coffee and tea. They did two things: they tricked me into thinking I was drinking plenty of water (because they're liquids), and they dehydrated me. Those beverages act like diuretics, you know, sucking water from tissues, rather than replacing it. (If I were a logger, I would have said that my skids needed greasing.) Water facilitates all my brain and body processes, and without enough of it, I can plan on being weary and muddle-brained. So too Elijah. After he had snoozed awhile, God's angel set a jar of water right by his head. Water, not coffee or cola. When the prophet awoke from his restorative sleep, he drank it.

Step three followed hot on the heels of step two: I avoided anything sugary or composed of highly refined food. No toaster pastries, cookies, or cinnamon rolls. Instead, I ate whole-grain cereals, fruits, vegetables, and lean meats or legumes. Because they don't send my blood sugar bungee-jumping, they helped me stay alert and energetic longer. An added plus: after a few days of eating that way, my cravings for the high-sugar/high-fat foods subsided. In Elijah's day, folks cooked with whole grains. When the angel set "bread baked over hot coals" alongside that jar of water, you can be sure it was dense, chewy, unsweetened, whole-grain, stick-to-your-ribs fare.

Before Elijah moved to step four, he repeated steps one through three a couple of times. As Scripture tells it, "He ate and drank and then lay down again. The angel of the LORD came back a second time and touched him and said, 'Get up and eat, for the journey is too much for you.' So he got up and ate and drank" (1 Kings 19:6–8). I liked that idea. If I had to rest for more than a day, so be it.

But then, once strengthened by sleep, water, and good food, both Elijah and I could travel. And that's step four: travel. Exercise. Moving my limbs. I called my dear friend Laura and went for a walk. The exercise began to chase away sluggishness, clear my thinking, and cheer me up. Elijah, most likely in much better shape than I, walked for forty days. Laura and I walked for forty minutes. Either way, Elijah and I were ready for step five.

The final stamina step sent us straight to the Lord. Elijah ended up seeing God on Mount Horeb. I met Him at my kitchen table, where I came to Him like a little girl. "Papa," I began—and the rest spilled into His ears only. Then I opened His Word and let Him feed and water my famished heart—just as He had tended my body.

I feel better now. Rested, fueled, refreshed. Those tasks aren't yapping so noisily. Because I feel replenished and well loved, I can hear their demands differently. I don't have to do everything for everybody, and I don't have to perform perfectly. God will fill in the gaps.

Meanwhile, I will practice my new stamina steps. Rigorously. I'll start by hitting the hay.

LITTERMATES

ONE AUGUST DAWN I ENTERED THE HEAVY WOODS A HALF mile north of Goose Ridge. The sun's first beams ricocheted off tree trunks, as maple leaves the size of hubcaps caught the light like so many green umbrellas. The forest's families had enjoyed a good season. A skunk's tall tail, arched like a question mark and trailed by three miniature, identical tails, waggled a course through the undergrowth. At daybreak, does browsed with their fawns. Bullfrogs groaned, raccoons chuckled, and nocturnal possums wandered back to their dens.

These woods, like so many in our area, bump up against pasture. And so it happened that our neighbor's sheep lived in a small, fenced clearing shaded by the tangle of forest. I appreciate sheep, and when I pass their field, I often linger, thinking of the sheep in Scripture and looking for my likeness in their obtuse, vulnerable ways. They were already up and grazing that morning, grabbing grass in a paintbrush rhythm that could have kept me there for hours.

Might have, too, if I hadn't spotted the cougars. At first I couldn't believe it, mainly because I saw two of them: one crouched smack in the middle of the road, fifty yards away, and the other twenty feet behind it at the edge of the shoulder. Cougars usually live solitary lives, so these guys surprised me. I froze—and watched them for a few seconds before first one, then the other, vanished into the brush.

Though their spots had long since disappeared, and they surely approached 75 pounds each, these cats were youngsters. When they leave their mother at about eighteen months of age, cougar littermates may stay together for another month or two before they stake out individual territories. That explained, too, why they were watching the sheep. Inexperienced cats don't have the hunting savvy of older ones, so they wander, bewildered, for a while—catching what they can. Even so, they rarely bother livestock or people. My neighbor never lost any sheep, despite the cats' proximity.

That year cougars tracked the plentiful deer and small game along many of the creeks that riddle Whatcom County. Reports of spottings shot up like flares in our community. Someone saw a big cat behind his raspberry shed; another watched one near the Loomis Trail bridge. Two landscapers saw one by the creek at the fairgrounds. Hunters talked about them at the sporting goods counter at the Coast-to-Coast store. Moms kept their kids away from riparian corridors, where the cats might lurk. People discussed shooting them, trapping and relocating them, or letting them be. My leanings landed somewhere between the last two options, with hope for peaceful coexistence between these fabulous cats and the people who increasingly share their range.

While I wouldn't want a mountain lion in my yard, I like knowing they're around. Where cougars thrive, all is well. The links of God's food chain are hooking together as they should. "The wild animals honor me," He said, "because I provide water in the desert and streams in the wasteland" (Isaiah 43:20). God has designed an intricate pattern of relationships in His creation, all of which depend upon one another to flourish. Cougars survive because they have what they need.

God has a healthy ecosystem in mind for us as well—an ordered world that meets our needs. Just as cougars depend on a supportive environment, with habitat and food supply in place to sustain them, our personal wellness—mental, emotional, physical, and spiritual—also benefits from a chain of healthy, interacting components. We know that without care for our bodies, our minds can fail us. When our relationships run amok, our emotions may take us captive. When we contaminate our thoughts, our hearts harden. And when we ignore God, we eventually starve. But with the Lord's help, we can break those damaging habits and patterns, and in so doing, replant our lifestyle's vegetation.

"Perhaps," you say, "but my life's fragments are running around like motherless pheasant chicks. I can't catch them, much less calm and nourish them. Where do I start?"

When I wonder that, I ask God, who tells me, "Do not fear, for I am with you; do not be dismayed, for I am your God. I will strengthen you and help you; I will uphold you" (Isaiah 41:10). He adds, "I will lead the blind by ways they have not known, along unfamiliar paths I will guide them; I will turn the darkness into light before them and make the rough places smooth" (Isaiah 42:16).

Ask Him to show you where to begin. At a pace you can tolerate, He will help you restore your habitat. Do what He says; your ecosystem will heal and bloom. Then watch for the wonderful cat of wellness.

FENDER BENDER

"HAVE YOU SEEN WHAT THEY DID TO THE CREEK?" MY HUS-
band Blake asked, moments before he drove our van toward
the guardrail. When I shook my head, he had U-turned
toward the bridge, a couple of miles downstream from Goose
Ridge. With the current coursing beneath us, he pulled over
and pointed. "They lowered the culvert and terraced the
stream. Now the salmon can pass through. See it?"

He was watching the water as he talked, and in his enthusiasm, let the van roll closer to the edge. Too close. Bumper
and rail ground together as the van slid along the rail and
jerked our thoughts back to the road. We gave each other that
"uh-oh" look before we climbed out to view the damage. Yep.
Seriously scraped.

I love him all the more for it. Though Tuesday will find me
at the auto body shop, for now that scrape reminds me of

Blake's way of navigating this life—and I don't mean his driving. He understands a pivotal concept: Healing often takes time. He celebrates each piece of restoration, whether of a salmon stream or of a person's life.

That's why he hit the guardrail. Hope distracted him. A length of our creek was functioning again! In 1950, Vince Crabtree saw dog salmon swim in these waters—right past his farm. Then new roads and faulty drains blocked their route. But one small section at a time, folks have restored the stream; spawning fish can now swim in from the Pacific, up the Nooksack River, and into that small tributary fed by springs from Goose Ridge.

I've seen Blake just as excited when a distant husband finally looks into his wife's eyes and smiles, or a too-busy dad plays baseball with his son, or a mama locked in depression's throes for months tenderly brushes her four-year-old daughter's hair. In them, he sees chunks of healing. Of hope. Bits which, piled together, help restore the stream of healthy living. Blake can spot them. In fact, he expects to see them. He, like the apostle Paul, is "confident of this, that he who began a good work in you will carry it on to completion until the day of Christ Jesus" (Philippians 1:6).

God will do that. Ultimately (though it may take a lifetime), we who trust Jesus will become like Him, with nothing wrong in us at all. He will restore our courses, our dying streambeds, even more splendidly than He will revitalize His earth. Paul explained: "The creation itself will be liberated from its bondage to decay and brought into the glorious freedom of the children of God" (Romans 8:21). That's awesome enough to distract any driver.

Imagine having this restored: the ability to love and be loved. Jesus hauls away our guilt, shame, and self-loathing, and replaces it with the clean fill of forgiveness and total acceptance.

Restored: self-control.

Restored: honesty with ourselves and others.

Restored: courage to make the right choices.

Acre by acre, year after year, He redeems us. Eventually, He completes us. Last week, for instance, a salmon finned in the shallows beside Vince Crabtree's farm. And his grandson saw it.

Mind Cud

Cows, like deer and goats, have four stomachs. All belong in a suborder of animals called *ruminants*, which means—in comfortable terms—that they all chew cud. Here's the physiology: When they graze or browse, food lumps down into their rumens (one of their stomachs), where protozoa and bacteria ferment it a bit. When the beasts take a break, they regurgitate that partially digested food, then chew it awhile more, readying it for passage to the other three stomachs—the reticulum, omasum, and abomasum. (Who thinks up these names?)

You will see what I mean if you do this: The next time you're driving in the country and pass a herd of cows, pull off the road, roll down your window, and watch awhile. Better yet, get out of the car and sit by the fence, where you can see them *and* hear them. If you wait long enough, you'll see the grazing herd, their bellies full of sweet grass, lie down to rest. Stand close enough, and you'll hear them burp—right before they begin pulverizing their forage.

I was raised in logging country, not around cattle. I guess that's why it never registered when my exasperated mom threw up her hands over the three sticks of Doublemint gum I'd stuff in my mouth all at once. "You're chewing that like a cud, Cheryl!" she'd exclaim.

I didn't mind. Even today, I consider gum-chewing an event—the noisier the better. But after watching cows, I don't chew just any old place. Knowing that my habit resembles bovine activity keeps me discreet.

Cows chew that cud hard, with big, circular swoops of their lower jaws. You can hear them grind, grind, grind, burp, pause, and grind some more.

Enough of that. I don't usually hang out that close to our cows, so I don't think about cud-chewing much. That's why it took our goat to shift my attention.

He wandered over for a head-scratching one evening—as I watched fresh water swirl into the trough. When my fingers tired, I shooed him off. He lay down about ten feet away, promptly burped, and began chewing.

A garden hose takes a while to fill a hundred-gallon trough, so I sat in the grass next to Goat to pass the time. He didn't even look at me; he just kept chewing—relaxed, and focused on whatever it is small, fat, pygmy goats think about at the end of the day.

His tranquility appealed to me. *Sundays should be like that,* I thought. We should chew mind cud. Think how much we would rest and relax if we ruminated on the previous week, thanking God for His care and forgiveness in the midst of it. After all, when God had finished creating, he "saw all that he had made, and it was very good . . . on the seventh day he rested from all his work. And God blessed the seventh day and made it holy, because on it he rested from all the work of creating that he had done" (Genesis 1:31, 2:2–3). He looked back at what He had completed the previous week and digested it, declaring it good!

I don't typically spend Sundays like that. Sure, I worship and try to spend a quieter day, but I am usually looking ahead to the coming week—planning, anticipating.

Goat reminded me that when I finish my work at week's end, I can turn around and see all the ways God has loved me through the week. I can digest His work in my life and learn from my mistakes. I can put on the brakes, plop onto a soft spot, and chew on His love for me.

I like that idea. I'm going to approach Sundays differently from now on. I may even chew on a few sticks of Wrigley's—just to remind myself.

RURAL ROUTES

EVERY YEAR OR SO, SOMEBODY SMASHES OUR MAILBOX. IT stands at the end of our long lane—easy prey for night marauders who routinely club every box on our road.

We all get pretty sick of it. Replacing those boxes is pricey—in both money and time. So folks have taken countermeasures. Randy Plagerman bought a one-piece box and pole contraption advertised as indestructible. The antagonists just ran it over. The Brisma clan built an elaborate wire and wood frame for theirs. The box survived without a scratch, but oh, the frame—mangled. Mr. Hudson, his jaw set and his lips thin-lined, told us how he encased his mailbox in concrete. That worked, I think, until a snowplow ticked it last winter.

One neighbor, a volunteer fireman returning home from a night call, stopped at his own box. Over the hill, he heard a resounding whack, hoots of laughter, then tires screaming. He pulled into his driveway, turned off his lights, and waited. Minutes later, a carload of teenagers, baseball bats in hand, careened toward his mailbox. He flicked on his emergency lights, and took chase. When those kids tried to hide on a dead end, he trapped them. The sheriff arrived shortly and hauled them in. Charges? Minor in possession, damaging federal property. For two years thereafter, nobody touched our boxes.

I wouldn't recommend our neighbors' methods. We took a different tack, and so far, it has saved our mailbox. Come to think of it, it has helped us endure other antagonists as well.

We decided to build a "flexible" mailbox—one with some give to it. We used the same old galvanized style that we always had, but anchored it to its platform with only two nails. What's more, we only drove them a half-inch into the wood. Now the box stays attached in all sorts of weather, but when a bat or pumpkin clobbers it, it flies off its post and lands in the field behind it. It has suffered a few minor dents on its launchings, but we handily pound those out and remount it. The results? Time and money saved, equanimity preserved.

We try to approach life's irritations the same way—flexibly. While we won't compromise on major issues involving our values or beliefs, we try to stay flexible on nonessentials, to give in where we can, unless to do so would cause harm. Just as our mailbox needn't argue with a bat wielded by intoxicated teenagers, neither must we quibble with folks for the sake of control or pride. "If it is possible, as far as it depends on you, live at peace with everyone. Do not take revenge, my friends, but leave room for God's wrath, for it is written: 'It is mine to avenge; I will repay,' says the Lord" (Romans 12:18–19).

Makes sense, doesn't it? After all, "A heart at peace gives life to the body" (Proverbs 14:30). Flexibility improves our health by contributing to our peace. Adaptable attitudes can help our bodies produce more serotonin, a neurotransmitter that promotes well-being. Too, a peaceful outlook reduces production of stress hormones, which can debilitate the body over time. When we aren't constantly battling people and circumstances over every little thing, we can save our energies for issues that have eternal significance, and we can free our minds to see God at work.

Like our mailbox, we have accumulated some dents over the years, and we have certainly gone flying a time or two. But we haven't been spiritually run over or mangled. Because we trust God, we needn't be rigid.

Two nails will do.

DRAGLINE

Last summer, old Bill Tyas dug out our pond. Years of clay silt had piggybacked on the fresh springwater filling it, and blackberries had hidden it from view. When he first looked it over, Bill shared our vision of a placid pool of sweet water, nestled at the base of the woods. He especially liked the spring's steady flow. No stagnant, smelly pond here. This one would host all the life a good pond should.

His heavy equipment arrived within the week. His bull-dozer bladed out berries and left the detached vines in a heap, where they would grow brittle and decompose. Painless enough. But for the real work, he needed his dragline and bucket, dangling from a crane that had crawled slowly across Goose Ridge and waited its turn at the pond's edge. Once Bill climbed into the crane's cab, the disturbing work began.

First he swung the crane arm out over the water, which

(with the blackberry brambles gone) reflected the azure sky and the leafy, overhanging alder branches. Then, with the flip of a round-knobbed lever, he dropped the bucket, weighted so that its teeth plunged into the pond's floor. When he tightened the attached cable, up came a bucket-load of black muck, with slurry streaming out of it. He piled the whole mess in a mound off to one side. For three full days he dropped and filled that bucket. I memorized the rhythm: swing, drop, lift, swing, empty; swing, drop, lift, swing, empty. A raw hole deepened daily, black mire mixed with blue clay, oozing and ugly. The spring's flow looked like a trickle dropping into that rotten mouth.

I hated it. I was sorry we had done it. Though Bill assured me that I would like the results, and though I knew I was overreacting, I was still dismayed. Even after he had smoothed the raw edge with an excavator, the ground still looked rutted and torn. The pond slumped deep—a collapsed, exhausted puddle. The mountain of seeping clay beside it compounded my upset. Before soil could be spread out and contoured, it had to dry a while so it wouldn't act like glue.

Bill finished that phase of the work and left to tend other jobs. For a week I mourned. But in that week, the pond filled. *Maybe,* I thought, *this will heal after all.*

It did, of course. Once the excavated material drained and dried a bit, Bill spread it around, and it virtually vanished. We cast grass seed over it all, which sprouted before the first frost.

Clay particles suspended in the water settled, and again its surface bounced the sky's blue upward. Creatures visible and microscopic populated the healthy, inviting pond.

Every so often I ask the Lord to drop His drag bucket into me. I pray the psalmist's prayer: "Search me, O God, and know my heart; test me and know my anxious thoughts. See if there is any offensive way in me, and lead me in the way everlasting" (Psalm 139:23–24). I dislike the process even more than I did the work on our pond. It hurts. But if I am willing to let Him, the Lord will haul out the sludge in my soul. You know what that is: pride, greed, bitterness, fear, envy, lust, resentment—all the lousy stuff that lurks in the depths. Sometimes He insists that I look at it awhile before He totes it off. He asks me to feel the pain it causes, to acknowledge my part in it, and to stop blaming others. I shudder over the whole miserable mess.

But I do like the results. He dredges me. Humility clears my mind. I can love and think more deeply. As He empties out my rotten muck, He fills me with his living water. Jesus promises, "Whoever drinks the water I give him will never thirst. Indeed, the water I give him will become in him a spring of water welling up to eternal life" (John 4:14).

Swing, drop, lift, swing, empty. It's worth it.

LEANINGS

At the house on Fifth Street, we burned wood—whether we liked it or not. All four of us, as soon as we were old enough to struggle a chunk of firewood into our arms, would load our wheelbarrow with it. One of us older kids would shove that iron-wheeled barrow to the cellar chute, strap open the hatch, and hurl firewood down into the basement where the insatiable furnace waited for us to feed it.

We hated that octopus furnace with its tentacle vents. It forced us into our dank basement, with its spiders and withered potatoes. The furnace enslaved us, because we needed its hot breath to blow through the grates upstairs. Winter mornings we dressed for school over those vents, stalling as our billowing nightgowns trapped warmth against our shivering bodies.

But because of that tyrannical furnace, we had a woodpile. And in a good woodpile, dreams take shape.

On the first Saturday of every month, we would hear the wood man drive into the alley. We knew his truck's rumble, its grinding gears. We would run outside just as he pulled up behind the garage. Without looking at us, he would strap on his wide belt, climb the slats on the sides of the flatbed, and crawl atop his load. Then he would pause and survey our faces, some smeared with jelly and toast crumbs, all waiting for the new wood. "Back up, now. Behind the fence, all of ya." We knew he would stare at us until we gathered behind the backyard gate—out of range of his flying logs.

They were honest-to-goodness logs, too—fir, alder, birch, maple, spruce—cut into the two-foot sections our deep-mouthed furnace swallowed. The loggers had split some of them, but most were round, with flat-sawn ends. Perfect for building.

Whenever we played with the wood, we entered an imaginary world, one in which my brother Vincent constructed mansions, using a few scraps of lumber for crossbeams and roofing, and stacked logs for walls. Inside his structure, sister Jan made grass-clipping beds for her many adopted "children." I set round logs on end—desks and stools for my "students." (I'd feed siblings and neighbors cookies if they would enroll.) My baby sister Dana decorated all our construction with fir cones and fiery red peonies that grew on a drooping bush by the smokehouse.

We didn't know it at the time, but we were all working out our dreams, practicing the blueprints God had for us. Our elders could have learned much by watching us in the woodpile.

When Solomon advised parents to "Train a child in the way he should go, and when he is old he will not turn from it" (Proverbs 22:6), he was encouraging us to help our children make decisions in keeping with who God created them to be. Of course, to do that, we must first introduce them to Jesus, and teach them about His salvation and wisdom for living. Next, we are to observe and acknowledge their God-given aptitudes and interests, the traits that will shape their future callings. When we can help direct and develop those innate leanings, we are helping those children grow into God's plans for them.

Anyone observing us children with eyes for our futures would have identified my brother's love of crafting raw materials into functional, beautiful objects. His hands were magic— even in the woodpile. Today he makes his living restoring antique tile roofs on historic buildings. For fun, he remodels his house and rebuilds classic cars. Sister Jan always talked of adopting children who needed homes, and practiced loving them as she played in the woodpile. Today she and her husband have five adopted children, for a total of seven well-loved kids. Baby sister Dana picked bouquets everywhere, when she could. When she couldn't find flowers or cones or shells to decorate with, she made them. She is still at it, creating and selling her artwork around the state. I continue to move desks around at school—and hand out cookies to my students.

Oh . . . and I teach them to write about their dreams.

BIRD NET

A WHILE BACK WE VISITED THIRD COUSINS JEAN AND Everett. Avid, artistic gardeners, they wrap their country house in a symphony of blooms. They fill feeders, too, with seeds like millet, sunflower, and sterilized thistle. Birds flock to their place as to a siren call—a sometimes deadly one. They don't see the glass enclosing the breezeway between house and garage, and consider it a flyway instead. Jean told how she cringed at the familiar thump of beak, head, and body hitting the window. Too frequently, she had retrieved broken-necked towhees, robins, pine siskins, or grosbeaks, crumpled in heaps beneath the sash.

. And so they hung lightweight nets. Everett suspended them a few inches away from the window, hoping they would arrest the birds before they crashed. At the very least, nets would soften impact.

By the time we visited, their yard's floral heyday was hosting a festival of birds who no longer died on exit. As Everett told it, those birds on errant flights bumped the net and simply flew off. Everett popped the net lightly with his hand, to demonstrate.

The net's wavelike movement drew my eye down, and my gaze landed on a crumpled leaf between glass and net. You should know that I'm mildly nearsighted. Without my specs, a distant sawhorse can resemble a deer. Maybe that explains why I reached under the net to brush away an old leaf, and instead found myself holding a female rufous hummingbird. In her limp state, her little green and rust feathers indeed looked like a wilted leaf.

I thought she was dead—another window victim. I gingerly held her in my palm, studying her thread-like feet, iridescent feathers, chin freckles.

Then she moved. She hadn't hit the window at all. She had found her way through the webbing of the net and been trapped. She had expended her fuel reserves trying to escape and had finally lain exhausted on the ledge.

We jumped into action. Everett unhooked a feeder hanging from the eaves—one of those red plastic doodads filled with red nectar. He set it on the picnic table, and I ever so gently poked her needle beak into one of the yellow holes at the center of the red plastic flower.

What a long shot, I thought as she lay there. But how else could we get her to drink? I jostled her. No, that's too strong a word. How does one jostle a hummingbird? I nudged her, then eased her beak further into the hole. She twitched. Then, almost imperceptibly, she started to sip. I felt her tremble. I moved her again, and she drank more vigorously this time. The tiny engine in her body started to vibrate as the liquid revved her mighty metabolism. For a few seconds more, she drank—enough to send a bubble rising through the feeder.

We crowded around the table, mesmerized, until with a whirring hum, she lifted vertically off my hand, hovered briefly, and zigged away.

On our three-hour drive home, I thought about that hummer: trapped, rescued, revived, and set free. I grinned at how God allowed one of his most fragile, exquisite creatures to reeducate slow, cotton-headed me. He reminded me of my days between the net and the glass, when faulty thinking trapped me in confines that kept me undernourished and unable to fly. When I lay exhausted on the bottom ledge, He sent folks to bring me out into the open, to feed me on His Word, and to hold me openhanded until I let God heave my trembling soul skyward. I experienced firsthand His promise: "Then you will know the truth, and the truth will set you free" (John 8:32).

It is amazing enough that He did it once. But in the years since, He's freed me often—from thinking I had to accomplish more than He had planned for me; from believing that achievements would bring me love; from pride and fear that were starving my relationships and my choices; from depending upon myself (rather than Him) to stay physically or emotionally safe. I am learning that salvation is more than my future life after death. In this life, too, He will repeatedly liberate me (if I let him) from situations or thoughts that can trap me like treacherous nets or deadly glass.

Before we got home, I found myself thanking God for the folks He sends to help untangle me when I fly into the webbing. And I asked Him to point me to others similarly trapped. With the scissors of the Word, and the hand of His Spirit, I can help snip them free.

So can you.

WINTER COATS

I COULD SELL TICKETS TO OUR ANNUAL DOG-SHAVING. ANYONE interested in drama, comedy, or psychology would stand in line to buy one. The production only lasts an hour and a half, but if you sat in the premium seats (our porch steps), you would be touched—by dog hair, at least. It would cover every inch of you.

Let me explain. Retrievers Rookie and Iceberg grow dense coats. Our winters can chill the hardiest hounds to the bone, and those dogs need that insulating fur. The thick undercoat keeps their skin completely dry as they swim, slog through swamps, and sniff along ponds and creeks. Water will not penetrate it.

But those coats do have disadvantages. They mat behind ears, harbor bugs and burrs, and smell downright terrible. Skin never sees the light of day. Often, bathing does little good, since both dogs—preferring their stinky state—find something ripe to roll in within forty-five seconds of rinse-off. And shedded hair will latch onto any dark clothing within fifty yards. Guaranteed.

So as soon as the weather warms up in the spring, I shave them. Poorly. My limited experience with electric clippers means that I get their hair off, but it isn't pretty. This year Rookie had bald spots on her neck and belly, mismatched tufts on her feet, and stripes on her back like those made in a lawn by a mower run amok. Iceberg, that ticklish boy, wouldn't let me finish his tail, so the left side got shaved and the right stayed hairy.

Oh well. They smell better afterwards. Most of that hair ends up in the trash, and when a shaved Rookie scratches, she can actually get at the itch.

This spring I clipped them on a warm evening. Our kids parked on the steps to watch as I barbered Iceberg. They observed silently as I made my first few passes. But the more those clumps fell to the ground, the more they commented. As the real Bergie emerged out of all that camouflaging fur, they laughed and chattered nonstop.

I know I'm clumsy with those clippers, but I still get the job done. When Iceberg trots away, his fur lies in puddles. He's free of the whole smothering, malodorous mop. As a result, he pants less from summer heat. He's cleaner. Because he doesn't stink, we don't shoo him away, and we enjoy him more.

Much of mothering resembles dog shaving, you know. Day after day, year after year, we groom our kids' character. When a child's undercoat of resistance thickens, we clip it with discipline, so that God's living water can reach the skin. When selfishness or dishonesty tangles and mats life choices, we do our best to shave it away. When topics are just too ticklish, we will leave them alone—and address them later.

God encourages us to keep barbering. But as we do, He cautions us, "Do not exasperate your children; instead, bring them up in the training and instruction of the Lord" (Ephesians 6:4). He tell us to "take note of this: Everyone should be quick to listen, slow to speak and slow to become angry, for man's anger does not bring about the righteous life that God desires" (James 1:19).

Parenting is a messy process, and awkward. We need God's grace and patience to do the job. Moms know that heart-shaving takes a long time. Plus, it requires both delicate sensitivity and bold strokes. Even when we give it our best effort and try to listen well, we can end up covered with emotional residue, and itchy. We may want to dump the clippers and go for a swim.

But let's not give up. Children respond to long-suffering love and discipline. Given that blend, their defenses can drop off, their consciences come clean, their attitudes improve. If we don't lose hope, they will be likely to open up and talk more, shedding some of life's stink.

Like Iceberg, they can trot away free.

A GREEN BOX

AN OVAL WOODEN BOX WITH A SNUG-FITTING LID SITS ON A shelf above my desk. My sister, Jan Soto, painted it dark green before she sent it to me. The day that box arrived in the mail, I took off its lid and loaded it with stones I had collected through the years—blue agate, opal, garnet, amethyst, tiger eye, tourmaline, jasper—all previously hidden underground, now polished and fabulous.

Her prayer made me fill it. She had composed and transcribed a few lines onto a small sheet of yellow paper, which she folded and tucked into in the bottom of the box. When I read her words, I knew she had seen my defensive heart—and was lifting it to the Father. She wrote,

> I keep my lid on—oh, so tight
> You coax it off. Why do I fight?

I put it back, but then I see
You've healed another part of me.
I feel so safe when shut inside.
No fears, no tears; they all can hide.
But then you lift the lid once more.
I argue so! My heart is sore.
Go slowly, Lord; stay close to me
I am afraid of what I'll see.
When that tight lid falls to the ground,
I feel my heart begin to pound;
I wonder if my fear will show.
Can I survive? I do not know.
You pick me up and wipe my tears;
You take away my awful fears.
There lies my box, and by its side
The lid is off. No place to hide.
Stay close, my Lord. I'm traveling through
These hidden feelings, deep and true.
My lid is off; I want to see,
To let you heal all of me.
Amen.

I look at that box nearly every day. I finger the lid sitting beside it, and the rocks it holds. I lift them to the light and marvel at their color, their construction, their density. I remember that if I clamped the lid into place, neither I—nor anyone else—would see the gemstones inside.

I need that mental picture and my sister knows it. Every chance she gets she encourages me to open up and grow deeper in Christ. Because I can be self-protective and anxious, she reminds me that God is trustworthy and gentle—and that I can let my guard down with Him. When I do, He prepares and extracts treasure from my depths, turning sharp-edged stone into polished gems. Even when all I see are those jagged edges, I can remember that He makes "everything beautiful in its time" (Ecclesiastes 3:11).

His Word assures me that He will handle my innards carefully. When I worry about facing my heart's recesses, He quiets me as He says, "The Spirit helps us in our weakness. We do not know what we ought to pray for, but the Spirit himself intercedes for us with groans that words cannot express. And he who searches our hearts knows the mind of the Spirit, because the Spirit intercedes for the saints in accordance with God's will" (Romans 8:26–27).

Remember that the next time you want to pack your heart in a box and close the lid. It's dark in there.

U-Turns

I KNOW MY WAY AROUND SACRAMENTO NOW. BETTER THAN I did, anyway. The last week of June, I hauled volleyball players (my daughter included) to tournament matches in that city—at remote courts with names like Spike City and Volleyball Café.

Finding those courts proved no easy task, mind you. From seats in our rented van, we read maps, asked for directions at the Exxon station, guessed, and took circuitous routes to our next game. We had considerable trouble with the concrete medians dividing opposing traffic lanes. They were everywhere; a driver couldn't just quietly turn left at any old street, much less change direction. I had to watch for openings at intersections before I could *maybe* turn left. Altering my route took planning . . . and time. I repeatedly felt trapped in asphalt chutes that wouldn't let me turn around.

But then I learned about U-turns. Sacramento practically celebrates them, you know. Where I live, we just "flip a yewie" when nobody's looking, and feel sneaky doing it. Not in Sacramento. There, they even have U-turn lights! When a little arrow in the shape of an upside down *U* turned green, I could curl around that median and drive the opposite way, while four lanes of traffic waited for me. Nothing furtive about these U-turns; I could wave and smile at those waiting cars, knowing I wasn't breaking any laws.

What a hoot. Yewies! Sanctioned by the authorities! I hadn't enjoyed running errands so much since I was sixteen years old, sporting my new driver's license. I gladly agreed to make extra pizza and water runs—as long as I could make a U-turn or two en route.

I'm not always so easily entertained, but those Sacramento U-turns reminded me of something. Whenever I cranked the steering wheel hard left, I thought of the freedom Christ gives me to change my course. Every time I made one of those wonderful turns—invited by that green arrow—I relived God's invitation to me when, as a college freshman, I badly needed a break in the median and a new direction. I recalled that turnaround, when I said, "Yes, Lord, I have been making a mess of things . . . and I am sorry." I remember praying, "Lord Jesus, I believe You died and rose again so that I could start over. Will You help me? Will You guide me now . . . and when the time comes, take me to heaven?" He held back traffic while I looped onto His road and accelerated toward Him, toward His freedom from old entrenched patterns of anxiety and sin.

The psalmist described my experience well: "In my anguish I cried to the LORD, and he answered me by setting me free" (Psalm 118:5). A chapter later, he wrote, "I run in the path of your commands, for you have set my heart free" (Psalm 119:32). Jesus offered the clincher: "So if the Son sets you free, you will be free indeed" (John 8:36).

I think about those promises as I study the map of God's Word. I'm still asking Him for directions, and even guessing now and then, but I do like His road. Those sanctioned U-turns really can set a person free . . . and not just in Sacramento.

OSPREY

WE SAW THE GIANT BIRD FLYING TOWARD US ACROSS THE valley. Just a speck still, he caught our attention anyway, his slow flap and high altitude telling us that this was no songbird. When we spotted him, Blake and I had settled into lawn chairs at the edge of the pond, watching swimmers. Our dogs were towing two kids—who lay belly-down on inner tubes— to the tiny island where geese had brooded earlier in the spring. Several other children floated and dunked each other, shrieking with laughter in the sultry summer heat.

"I think it's an eagle," I said, wishing for binoculars.

"Maybe." I could practically see Blake's brain cogs turning as he studied the approaching bird.

Within minutes, it had settled into a circling pattern, a hundred feet above the pond. Still a silhouette, it mystified me. Neither Blake nor I spoke.

Then the bird started to drop. Gradually he lost altitude, his slow spiral bringing him close enough for us to see him better. He was certainly a large raptor, about the size of an eagle. But I had never seen those markings. A large white triangle extended across his underbelly and wings. Black streaks emanated back from his eyes on an otherwise white head. No eagle looks like that.

"I think it's an osprey," Blake decided.

By the time we could see all of this, the bird had continued to circle, drop, and circle. His head was cocked to one side as he studied the water. He meant business. We called the kids to shore.

No sooner had they left the water than the bird descended to within thirty feet of the pond's settling surface. Even the children were quiet now, all of us transfixed on the hunting osprey. Trout grow fat in that pond; the bird wanted them.

We could tell that he had spotted one when he hovered, wings pounding, legs trailing beneath him. Suddenly he dropped straight down, his talons and head projected toward the water. With wings extended vertically and tail spread, he plunged into the drink, snatched the unsuspecting trout, and flapped back into the air . . . all in a blink or two.

I almost fell backwards in my chair, I was so excited. But if I had, I would have missed what came next. Quickly the osprey rose to about fifty feet, where he again hovered. As he hung there, he shifted the fish's position so that its head pointed forward—"an aerodynamically efficient position," Blake said. With the fish secured, he flapped higher into the air and back across the valley. We watched until he disappeared in the distance.

I spent the rest of the evening with my bird book, reading up on raptors in general, ospreys in particular. I was trying to reconstruct the big bird's destination after he flew away from us. I suspect that he carted the fish home to his sprawling, messy nest, where he fed it to three nestlings who probably lived there. Quite a place, that nest. I learned that since the parents added to its mass each year, it could weigh up to half a ton—and could be built of branches, old boots, garden tools, fishnet, bones, and other trash—a bit of a slum, actually.

For a couple of days, it was all I could talk about. If I hadn't quieted down, folks would have started avoiding me, whispering, "Here comes that osprey woman," as they scuttled out of sight.

Eventually, I started remembering all the ospreys I had seen through the years. Well, not actually ospreys, but people who resemble them. Bear with me here; I don't mean adults with striped feathers. I am talking about the apparently strong, capable folks who soar through our days, and who seem to have no need for Christ. But at night, they fly home to messy nests—disordered, trash-filled lives. I used to be one of those birds myself.

But at some point those raptors get hungry. If they are true spiritual ospreys, sooner or later they plunge toward Jesus Christ and believe Him when He says, "He who comes to me will never go hungry" (John 6:35). They catch up the gospel and grip it. Then they haul it home and feed on it with their children.

I thought, too, of us swimmers, so busy with our own pursuits that we may ignore the big human birds circling nearby. We may not recognize their hunger, their need for a clear path to Jesus Christ.

The osprey convicted me. I asked God to help me live so that I would not float aimlessly, and in so doing block another's path to the Savior. I prayed that my behavior would match the faith I profess. Finally, I asked that He would help me spot hungry people, and show me how to offer them direct flights to Him.

Their splash can knock a person over.

OLDER

THE VULTURES IRRITATED ME. I WAS LYING ON THE GRASS
watching summer clouds transfigure themselves when I spotted the creatures circling high overhead, riding the updrafts, and
eyeing me. Now if they had been hawks or eagles, I wouldn't
have taken offense, but these were turkey vultures—cocking
their bald red heads so they could check out my carcass.

Ugly things, I thought. Just the week before, we had seen
five of them dismantling a dead heifer in Groen's field. Lying
so still, I must have looked like another tasty goner. They were
planning to tidy up our yard, I'm sure.

I didn't like that. I jumped up and hollered at them. "Not
yet, you guys. Wrinkled? Yes. Finished? Hardly!" My son, eating a sandwich by the kitchen nook window, rolled his eyes at
his mother, out there shouting at nobody. The vultures flew
off to find a quieter meal.

How times have changed. As a younger woman, I wanted to look gorgeous. Interpretation: I wanted other people to find me attractive. So I spent a good bit of time, energy, and thought on hair, clothes, makeup—the outer accoutrements that people seem to like so much. Now and then, I could turn heads.

But years passed. I can't pull it off anymore. It seems that the only heads I turn these days belong to vultures noticing my potentially decaying flesh. Despite reasonable exercise, my weight has migrated—to my middle, my hips. Years ago I asked a clerk in the junior department to help me find some slacks. "For you?" she asked. When I nodded, she gently pointed me toward the misses' racks.

Too, my eyes have collapsed. Well, the skin around them has. I hadn't minded the crow's feet (laugh lines, you know), but when the tissue under my eyebrows surrendered to gravity, it began to drape like a window swag. My eyes now look half their youthful size.

Another treachery: My skin has rebelled against tanning. Marathon sessions in the sun as a teenager (armed with baby oil and spray bottle) had, as the prophets promised, caught up with me. Now significant sun exposure leaves me mottled, freckled, crinkled—not a pretty sight.

Eventually, all the tools that had enabled me to compete in this culture's arena of physical acceptability lost their edge. My idols weren't working for me as they once did. I had two choices: I could try harder to earn approval given to the young and lovely, even if that meant snipping and dyeing, suctioning and implanting. Or, I could let it go—but not by opting for gluttony, inactivity, loss of hygiene, or army surplus duds. Instead, I could enjoy the view from this stage of life—safe and treasured as an older woman in God's hands.

Uh-oh. I hear someone who has had cosmetic surgery bristling. Please don't. God doesn't nix those improvements for everyone. It's just that for me, right now, they would steal my peace. Longing for youthful beauty—and fervently seeking it—would distract and enslave me, locking my eyes on earthly attractions, making me more competitive than loving, and keeping me afraid of the temporary physical decline that will culminate at heaven's door. If I were to act on that fear, I may even feed the fear of others struggling with their own physical changes.

Because of God's love for me, I don't need to worry about the loss of my youth. I no longer have to waste time trying to look good in order to be accepted. Aging prods me to quit proving myself, and to let myself move in the freedom of God's approval. "Listen to me," God says in Isaiah 46:3–4, "you whom I have upheld since you were conceived, and have carried since your birth. Even to your old age and gray hairs I am he, I am he who will sustain you. I have made you and I will carry you; I will sustain you and I will rescue you." In Psalm 92:14, He said that we "will still bear fruit in old age," and we "will stay fresh and green." In those words I hear Him saying that I will stay loved and valuable even if I don't resemble an emerging rosebud.

God knows that "charm is deceptive, and beauty is fleeting; but a woman who fears the LORD is to be praised" (Proverbs 31:30). By concentrating on Him instead of on my own advancement, He will build into me the "unfading beauty of a gentle and quiet spirit, which is of great worth in God's sight" (1 Peter 3:4). That beauty has no constraints of time or genetics.

I liked being young, and I miss it sometimes. But I have quit looking backward and longing for what is gone. In so doing, I have found the freedom to embrace each day—no matter how old I grow.

Even if vultures hover.

THE FENCE

WHEN MY HUSBAND, BLAKE, WAS IN COLLEGE, HE SPENT ONE summer building elk fences across the Wenas country in eastern Washington. It was hard work. He fought rocky soil, sagebrush, and high heat. He killed rattlesnakes with his shovel. But along the way, he learned to build fences that would last.

After we were married, he put up fences around our first two homes: solid, strong, straight fences. Twenty years later, they still stood.

Three years ago, we started yet another—a horse fence around our west pasture and paddock. Since we sandwiched construction time into busy Saturdays and occasional days off, work progressed slowly—until the summer of '98. A community of friends arrived early one morning, ready to work. Festively, they planted more than a hundred wooden posts. No longer did the project's end seem so elusive and overwhelming.

We only needed to brace a few more corners and string vinyl-coated wire between the posts before we could call it done.

Well, summer skipped into fall, fall begat winter, and then winter passed before we mustered enthusiasm to work on the fence again.

When spring break arrived, our family work crew looked to Blake for instruction. He gave each of us a different task. I unrolled, measured, and cut wire, then attached it to the corner posts. Avery measured and marked wire positions for Andrew, who positioned the wire and nailed in the anchoring staples. Blake cemented posts, and braced and drilled corners.

At first we were crabby. We fussed and grumbled at uncooperative wire—and at each other. What a lousy way to spend a vacation! Names of relaxing destinations escaped our muttering lips. I think I heard the word *Hawaii* drift between my son and daughter five or six times.

But we stuck with it. As the fence went up, we calmed down—and got better at our assignments. The wire had fewer kinks in it, and we started to focus on the quality of our work. We cared not just about getting the job done, but about having a straight, strong fence. We gradually got into a rhythm, and urged each other on.

That week now stands as one of my favorite vacations. ("You're nuts, Mom," commented a teenager reading over my shoulder as I wrote this.) But I mean it. God used the fence-building to clarify one of my prayers as a mother.

My heart's desire is that at the end of their lives, our children will be able to say, like Paul did to Timothy, "I have fought the good fight, I have finished the race, I have kept the faith" (2 Timothy 4:7). Building fences can help them do that by teaching them that building, whether fences or lives, is difficult. But even with the balky material we are all made of, they can learn to construct godly, loving relationships across varied emotional terrain—some lush, some barren, some fertile, some rocky.

Also, the fence demonstrated the importance of living with the end in sight. Once we decided to build a durable, straight, handsome fence (and not to just get the dumb thing up), we built it knowing we wanted to look back on the finished work and say, "Well done." The project modeled an attitude that I pray will permeate our children's choices.

I want them to decide to build their lives on God's love, to know that just as they looked to their dad for guidance on the fence, so too can they look to the Lord for direction. Not only will the Word show them how to live, but our God will help them follow his instructions—by the power of His Holy Spirit. When energy flags, He will send friends alongside to help. When they feel like quitting, the family of God will urge them on. And when they plant a crooked post, His grace will straighten it.

Their lives will be good to look back on.

FROG-TOTING ANGELS

THIS IS A HORRIBLE STORY—OR A WONDERFUL ONE, DEPEND-ing upon how you look at it. And that is the very point of telling it.

Every summer for twelve years, we went camping with several other families. To prepare, we would load tents, portable stoves, sleeping bags, axes, clotheslines, towels, lanterns, food—all sorts of necessary and unnecessary paraphernalia—into vehicles. Then we would drive caravan-style to campgrounds east of the Cascade Mountains, where warm weather, water sports, and lots of room pretty much guaranteed a memorable time for us adults and our assorted kids—up to thirty-five of them.

One summer we traveled across Highway 2 to a campground a few miles north of Wenatchee—a place called Lincoln Rock. After riding in cars for four hours, setting up camp, and gulping spaghetti and watermelon, the pack of grade-schoolers in our midst was clamoring for a baseball game. Amid hoots and taunts, we broke into teams: kids versus adults. Two teams with very different skill and energy levels. All strengths considered, an even match.

Except that the umpire was a dad. Because his age profile matched that of us old folks, the eight- to ten-year-olds in the group happily viewed his motives as suspect and protested every call. "No fair, Ump! You're on *their* side!" they shouted repeatedly. They worked themselves into a frenzy; we returned to camp with a mob of hyperactive competitors.

At bedtime, they still hadn't settled down. In the tent next to ours, our son, Andrew, and two friends raised a ruckus long after others had fallen asleep. Finally, when they dropped off, we rested too.

About 2:30 in the morning, someone fumbling with the zipper on our tent awoke me. It was Andrew, trembling. "I got lost," he stammered. By now my sleep-fog was clearing. Both Blake and I sat up and looked at him, unprepared for what we were about to hear.

Apparently, after drifting into a fitful sleep, Andrew had gotten up to find a rest room. In the unfamiliar setting, he had no sense of his surroundings. As he told it, "I must have walked and walked, 'cause I woke up on the highway out by the store." I shuddered as a cold dread moved through me. That store was a good half-mile away, in a questionable area on a state highway. He was eight years old and out there alone at two o'clock on a Saturday morning.

He went on: "I stood by the road and called, 'Help, anybody. Help!' Nobody heard me. I started walking again and saw the gate to the park. When I got inside the park grounds, I saw two teenagers, who came up to me. One of them had a big bullfrog in his hands. When I told them I was lost, they showed me the frog and walked with me until we saw our tents. Then they left."

That was it. The whole story. I wrapped the little guy in a blanket and curled my arms around him. He fell right to sleep. I lay awake for hours, holding him.

At first I was terrified. Anything could have happened to him! Why hadn't we heard him leave his tent? He was only six feet and two thin tent walls away from us.

My initial fears convinced me to keep him in our tent every summer thereafter until he was twenty.

But as the night wore on, I heard God's comfort. Psalm 34:6–7 sang in my head. I thought of how Andrew had "called, and the Lord heard him; he saved him out of all his troubles." The angel of the LORD described in those verses had indeed encamped around him and delivered him. Later, I recalled God's promise of an angel to the Israelites, words that captured the night's events: "See, I am sending an angel ahead of you to guard you along the way and to bring you to the place I have prepared. Pay attention to him and listen to what he says" (Exodus 23:20–21).

I fell asleep just before dawn, but only after realizing that for the rest of my life, I would have nights like this, nights where I could either choose to fear for our children or to trust God with them. The first choice would lead me into controlling, pessimistic, anxious behavior, while the second would teach me to surrender them to God—who loves and cares for them perfectly. The outcome of the second choice? Optimistic parenting, flexibility, hope for their futures.

The next morning we looked for the boys who had helped Andrew back to camp. No one knew anything about those angels, wandering with a bullfrog in the darkest hours of the night. No one except the Father and us.

SOLUTIONS

ICEBERG THINKS AN OLD SOCK WILL SOLVE ANYTHING. When I'm unloading groceries, that 105-pound golden retriever will try to lighten my load by offering me that sock. As I enter hour two of hedge trimming, he'll plan to soothe sore muscles by trotting over with the good-as-liniment sock. Seeing me frown as I pitch soiled straw out of stalls, he delivers the mood-soother: a worn, size 12 . . . you guessed it . . . athletic sock, original color unknown.

We had a Shetland pony once—Ladybug—who heard me crying in the barn after my grandfather died. In she came with her own solution: a soft muzzle and warm scent. She gave up grazing to nudge me, then stood nearby—as grief curled me in the corner of her stall.

My husband brings me solutions, too. For twenty-five years, he has offered his patient analysis and problem-solving expertise for everything from paint colors to child-rearing to time management issues. I love him for it.

But you know, even the kindest critters and the most thoughtful husband cannot solve everything. Sometimes only women friends will do. Maybe that's why women's ministries mean so much to me.

At our church Bible study seventeen years ago, I got to know Becca. Her life had taken her into the misery the psalmist referred to variously as "the pit," "the floodwaters," "the miry depths." But the Lord had brought her out intact. Not only did she survive; she could talk about it. What's more, she had grown wiser and stronger and more in love with the Lord because of it!

Over time, her peace and hope told me the Lord was laying her woes to rest. She wasn't just a victim of tough circumstances who was mouthing empty "God talk." My own eyes and ears told me she was truly being set free from the death stench that permeates disaster and that can poison us with fear, hatred, or hopelessness more far-reaching than the original tragedy.

She gave me courage. If God could release her from the clutches of her grim events, what was I waiting for? Our Christ-soaked friendship began for me a healing of wounds I had carried far too long.

Women can do that for each other—if they get together, and if Christ moves in their midst. That is why the enemy wants us to stay isolated, to stay away from the profound fellowship that women can offer one another. Those relationships can serve as conduits for the Holy Spirit's loving, healing, and empowering.

But when we are too busy or timid or discouraged for Bible study or small groups, the enemy gives his dirty servants a high-five. He has incapacitated us by keeping us alone, disconnected, and less effective.

Don't let that serpent trick you. Instead, ask God to provide a way for you to join a women's ministry. Ask Him for the time to fit it in—or for the courage to seek it out. Then ask Him to show you a ministry that is right for you. Groups like Bible Study Fellowship and Mothers of Preschoolers (a.k.a. MOPS) are just two of many good groups with national and international chapters. Churches offer Bible studies, as well as groups addressing everything from codependency to weight loss.

Finally, if you have never participated in a group before, ask God to quiet your anxieties about meeting new friends or about addressing topics that may stretch you. Don't worry. No one will wrench your story from you. Just go.

Let yourself be loved by a circle of friends. You might even come home with an old sock.

TRACKING AN ANT

A LOW, LUMPY CLOUD MAT HAD SETTLED LIKE A DIRTY sponge over Goose Ridge—and for 104 days it had dripped on us. For more than three months we had been awakening to a dim, monochromatic world that cried for color and a glimpse of sunshine.

One morning all four of us came to the breakfast table trailing the ends of our ropes.

"Enough rain already," someone said.

"I'm growing gills," said another. A third just plunked his head on the table, narrowly missing his Cheerios. So that day I—equally desperate—located some inexpensive tickets to Arizona; we flew south three days later.

The morning after our arrival, I trailed behind my daughter as she headed for the pool. I don't know whether the seventy-five-degree sunshine had already resuscitated her or whether she just wanted to try out those gills before they shriveled in the dry Tucson air. For whatever reason, she doffed her towel and jumped in the water.

I didn't follow. While she floated happily, I settled onto a chaise to read, still clad in long pants and a light sweater. Unaccustomed to the bright glare, I decided to lie on my stomach. I flattened the recliner and hung my chin over the end. That way, I could read the magazine as it lay on the shaded ground beneath me. Much better.

But then an ant crawled across the page. I quit reading and watched him. About three-eighths of an inch long, and packing a sesame seed off someone's hamburger bun in his jaws, this fellow looked like a rough harvester ant, a worker from one of the ground nests that riddle the sandy desert.

He knew where he was going. He was traveling due southeast, and my magazine didn't stop him. He angled his way to the page's edge, and descended to the aggregate pavement. I sat up and peered at him between my knees.

Before long he approached a nearby planter, loaded with blooming succulents. How would he traverse this? He paused, felt its edges, and went around it. But he didn't dodge a swimmer's sandal, lying on its side by a chair. He climbed straight up the leather straps and straight down its sole before continuing on his route.

"What are you doing, Mom?" my daughter called from the pool. By this time I had left my perch and was following the ant.

"Just watching an ant," I replied. I dropped to my knees and followed it under a table.

"Oh." She turned away and quickly ducked under the water.

After half an hour of progressing over and around man-made obstacles, he left the pool area. I climbed the low wrought-iron fence after him. He was traveling across sand now, between a prickly pear and a saguaro. For another forty-five minutes he persevered—crossing other ant trails, climbing stones and stems, skirting cacti. He must have passed the entrances to six or seven ant nests, ignoring them completely. At last he approached a small hole, only a half-inch in diameter, through which dozens of ants scurried. Without changing his pace, he dropped into the opening, and out of sight.

I straightened my bent-over frame and walked back to the pool, thinking about God and ants. "Go to the ant," the Lord says. "Consider its ways and be wise!" (Proverbs 6:6). Well, I had been considering his ways for more than an hour. Was I wiser? Maybe. I had seen that this tenacious crawler had *home* in mind. No matter what cropped up in front of him, and though he carried a load bigger than his head, he traveled steadily over terrain that could have blocked or confused him. Feet could have flattened him or birds swallowed him, but he followed the trail, knowing that it would lead him home if he just kept going.

Our trail leads home too—if we stay true to Christ's faith-map when obstacles like apathy, criticism, doubt, or difficulty loom. James puts it in eternal terms: "Blessed is the man who perseveres under trial, because when he has stood the test, he will receive the crown of life that God has promised to those who love him" (James 1:12).

We can trust that Christ will lead us through the desert to our eternal home with Him. And it will be much more inviting than an Arizona ant's nest.

EYESIGHT

THE YEAR WE HATCHED FORTY-EIGHT EXOTIC-BREED CHICKS in our incubator, we ended up with Small, a white hen with so many feathers over her eyes that she resembled a tiny mop. We doubted that she could see a thing, and so attributed her behavior to blindness. And that was true, in a way; the poor bird lacked common sense.

Ever at risk, she stood under our resting horses' bellies, in the path of oncoming cars, out in the open during rainstorms. She pecked at sleeping cats' tails. My high-pitched "Heeeere chick, chick, chick, chick" typically brought a waddling stampede of assorted fowl scurrying around the barn for the grain I'd scatter. But Small never caught on, never realized that she could go around the obstacle (barn) to the voice (food).

Our kids, preschoolers then, thought of her as a most convenient toy. Avery would plunk her in a doll carriage, cover her with a blanket up to her beak, and wheel her around the yard on many an afternoon. Best of all, Andrew could tuck the docile hen under one arm, climb to the top of our eight-foot slide, and launch Small down the waxed chute. The hen lay on her side the whole way down, until Avery would catch her at the bottom and carry her back to Andrew for another trip. The bird remained, literally, unruffled and oblivious.

She wandered too. When her reasonable colleagues retreated to roost at sunset, I would find her halfway down a row of raspberries, hopelessly lost. A few times, when she didn't show up, I called the neighbors. Once, an elderly lady a quarter mile from our house told me in broken English that she had locked Small in her woodshed when, after dark, the little hen had stood in her driveway, just looking around.

Sad to say, she never did learn any chicken wisdom. We think she eventually followed a nice-looking coyote home for dinner.

Last year I had a student who reminded me of Small. Katelyn repeatedly wandered, unthinking, into compromising and sometimes dangerous situations, where she would linger, lost, and unaware of the peril. She ignored Christian friends who genuinely cared about her, and instead meandered into relationships with "coyotes" who were waiting for the chance to devour her. Her foolishness left her defenseless.

That girl had us quaking, so a few of us teachers started praying for her. We asked the Lord to give her a hunger for

Himself and His wisdom. We knew that if she would turn to the Father, He would guard her course and protect her way. We claimed for her God's promises from Proverbs:

> Then you will understand what is right and just and fair—every good path. For wisdom will enter your heart, and knowledge will be pleasant to your soul. Discretion will protect you, and understanding will guard you. Wisdom will save you . . . Then you will go on your way in safety, and your foot will not stumble; when you lie down, you will not be afraid . . . for the LORD will be your confidence and will keep your foot from being snared. (Proverbs 2:9–12; 3:23–24, 26)

We can't wait to see what happens. Over the years, as we've prayed for other kids, we've seen God answer those prayers with his astounding, fabulous "Yes!" We've learned never to assume that someone is too foolish, too hardened, or too wounded for God to help. That's why we will never give up. We won't quit praying for Katelyn, even though she is still straying. We believe that someday she will run around the barn . . . straight toward Jesus' voice.

WEB KEEPER

THROUGH NO FAULT OF HER OWN, THE FAT SHAMROCK SPIDER was crawling in my hair. I had climbed between two strands of barbed wire, and burst, cheek-first, through her web. Now, with one hand still holding down the wire beneath me, I was brushing sticky wisps off my face. Meanwhile, I snagged my jacket on the wire stretched across my back. Before I could extricate myself, the spider, who was frantically trying to gain her footing, crawled from my bangs onto my forehead.

As much as I like spiders, she was too close . . . *much* too close. I shrieked and started shaking my head. I let go of the wire I was straddling and pawed at my face with both hands. Barbs from above and below sandwiched me into the fence. I panicked. I heard my clothing tear as I wrenched free from the wire, flung the spider into the grass, and flopped to the ground in a heap.

Fortunately, no one saw me but my dog, who barked at the unseen threat, then licked my face as I lay in the grass. If my kids had been watching, I would have heard them teasing, no doubt about it. "So a *spider* creeped you out, huh, Mom? I thought spiders were our *friends!*"

I did not feel like defending spiders at that moment. The memory of eight hairy legs dancing across my brow would have tainted my view—and unraveled my years of support for the little crawlers.

I have campaigned long and hard for the harmless spiders around here. When they show up in the bathtub, I lobby for relocation rather than squishing. When hundreds of tiny yellow spider babies hatch out of an egg sac glued safely under the eaves all winter, I rejoice—and stop whatever I am doing to watch them toss up silk sails that will haul them over the pasture and into the woods beyond. I have led sleepy young children outside on early summer mornings to see dozens of dew-beaded orb webs strung between tree branches, fence posts, and stalks of orchard grass. In my more supportive moments, I have even tossed a few buzzing houseflies into those sticky traps.

Through the window of my study, I once watched a spider build an orb web. Surprisingly, it took her less than an hour, from start to finish. Between an alpine fir's branches, she first attached a silken, polymer frame, complete with spokes that resembled those of an old, wooden, oxcart wheel. At the center, she threaded a stabilizing hub. (I reached out the window and touched it with the tip of my pencil; it wasn't sticky.) Then she connected glue-covered strands to each spoke, methodically forming the web that spiraled outward from the hub. A high-protein snack break followed; she returned to the hub she had woven at the web's center and ate it! Finally, she spun a signal thread, hooked it to her perch in the nearby branch, and waited. Within minutes, an errant crane fly flew into the trap. His struggles triggered a wobbling vibration in the signal thread that sent her scurrying after her prey.

Pretty neat. Not only did she build that intricate web out of silk from her own body, but also God told her just how to align it to intercept any insects headed her way. I liked the design so much I found myself wishing I had ears like webs. Only they would be oriented toward God's truth, not bugs, and sticky enough to lock onto his wisdom and encouragement. Whenever God-propelled words flew my way, they would lodge in my ears and set off a vibration in my soul that would send me scrambling to those nets for sustenance.

Come to think of it, maybe I already have them. After all, King Solomon seemed to understand how to position ear-webs to intercept God's Word. "Accept my words," he wrote, "and store up my commands within you, *turning your ear to wisdom* and applying your heart to understanding" (Proverbs 2:1–2, emphasis added). Even Isaiah wrote about ear-webs, when he said, "How gracious he will be when you cry for help! . . . Whether you turn to the right or to the left, your ears will hear a voice behind you, saying, 'This is the way; walk in it'" (Isaiah 30:19, 21). Later, that prophet described how God himself equips our ears: "He wakens me morning by morning, wakens my ear to listen like one being taught. The Sovereign LORD has opened my ears, and I have not been rebellious; I have not drawn back" (Isaiah 50:4–5).

And God's signal thread runs straight to my soul.

SLIPPERS

A PRESSED LADY'S SLIPPER SLID TO THE FLOOR THIS MORN-
ing. My grandmother had flattened it between the pages of
a book on wildflowers—before she passed the book on to
me. When I pulled it from the shelf this morning, the flower
fell out.

I wasn't surprised. Gram loves flowers. Even today—at
ninety years old—she returns from her walks with wonderful
specimens. To preserve them, she hides them in the pages of
the nearest book, capturing color and traits for us to marvel
over and study on cold winter days. Nearly every volume she
has ever given me has a garden tucked inside, mementos of
outings to remote Washington hillsides and Alaska shorelines.

When I was a child, Gram took us "slippering" every April.
Siblings, parents, grandparents, and aunts would bundle into
rain gear and load the trunk with shallow cardboard boxes

and shovels. Someone would throw a camera onto the dashboard. Then, overdressed and overcrowded, we would climb into a couple of vehicles and head for the Elwha watershed—an hour's drive away.

Despite the discomfort, few complained. After all, we were going to hunt wild orchids, and only in early spring's brief window could we find them. As we shouldered shovels, I felt like a prospector heading into the flower mines—those dim depths in the Olympic Peninsula's old-growth forest. We spread out in teams of two or three, climbing over ancient, rotting logs that now nursed litters of hemlock saplings. Trillium and yellow violets threw their color at us, but we traipsed past them. Finally, one of us would spot an orchid snugged into deep shade—and would let out a celebratory hoot.

Delicate as breath, a lady's slipper springs from a tiny bulb, embedded in forest duff beneath heavy moss. It clings there by a few weblike root fibers, so fragile that even the most careful, well-meaning child uproots it if she tries to pick the single purple blossom. Experts claim that those diminutive plants cannot be transplanted. Since their survival depends upon a nutrient exchange with soil fungi, they almost always die if disturbed.

But Gram made surgeons of us. Slowly, deliberately, she showed us how to excise the bulb and the soil around it—a huge shovelful—so that the bulb, roots, and flower remained undisturbed. As one of us lifted the shovel and its cargo, another slid the box beneath it, until the flower and its bedding could be settled into the box like a newborn into a crib.

Our digging done, we loaded our fragrant cargo into the trunk as carefully as we would handle loose eggs. If we wanted our slippers to survive, we needed to transplant them as tenderly as we had dug them.

We did. We lifted orchid boxes gingerly from the car trunk to sites at the base of two-hundred-year-old firs on the hillside below our grandparents' house. There we settled them. We eased each assembly—flower, stem, bulb, soil, fungi—into a scooped-out hollow.

They lived. Quite a few of them did, anyway. The year I left for college, Gram told me that the hillside under those fine old trees boasted a "closetful of slippers."

As I picture them now, those blossoms speak to me about more than my grandmother's successful instruction in botany. All the while she was showing us how to move those orchids out of the gloom, she was repeatedly demonstrating the tenderness Christ offers us—as He uproots us and replants us into His kingdom. "A bruised reed he will not break," says Isaiah 42:3. So gently, He cradles us frail ones into "the kingdom of light. For he has rescued us from the dominion of darkness" (Colossians 1:12–13).

Gram showed us that in His care, we—who are sometimes as fragile as lady's slippers, and who can "wither away like grass" (Psalm 102:11)—bloom.

SQUALL LINES

MUCH OF THE YEAR, WEATHER TRAFFIC RUNS HEAVY IN THE highway that stretches above Goose Ridge. Air masses constantly collide overhead, forming the fronts that shake up our forecasts. Only the bravest of couples plan weddings outdoors around here, huddling in a few squares on the late summer calendar. If they wait too long, they risk doing battle with squalls— those lines of fast, scowling, black clouds that have been known to rip light airplanes to pieces. Those storms look like sooty, churning ghosts, furiously beating the earth with ropes of rain.

When I see a squall line racing toward us, I fly out the back door and call children inside. Next, I shut the horse and goat in the barn. They know what's coming and are usually waiting for me at the gate. I whistle the dogs into the garage and call the cats to a warm sofa. Are the car windows rolled up? I check. I move lawn furniture to the lee side of the house, lest it tumble down the hill. Buckets, dog bowls, balls—anything loose in the yard, I retrieve, unless I want to track it down a hundred yards away after the storm.

When a squall approaches, I don't want to be vulnerable or exposed. I zip up clothing, tie down goods, and retreat to shelter. I protect my loved ones and the creatures in my care. Nasty weather is nothing to mess with.

But I am ashamed to admit that I have copied squalls from time to time. No, I haven't kicked buckets or knocked over furniture, but I have stormed into a room and sprayed my opinions on my children. I have sent them running for emotional cover by speaking before listening, and then by hearing only what I wanted to. When irritated, I have carried a low trough of pressure into rooms that could have been filled with grace, had I chosen tenderness instead.

A perceptive person once said that most of the friction of daily life is caused by the wrong tone of voice. He must have known about squall lines. So does the sage of Proverbs, who cautions, "When words are many, sin is not absent, but he who holds his tongue is wise" (Proverbs 10:19). In Proverbs 12:18, he adds, "Reckless words pierce like a sword, but the tongue of the wise brings healing." Read on. These verses convicted me to the bottom of my choppy mental sea.

> The wise woman builds her house, but with her own
> hands the foolish one tears hers down (Proverbs 14:1)

A gentle answer turns away wrath, but a harsh word stirs up anger (Proverbs 15:1)

Kind words heal and help; cutting words wound and maim (Proverbs 15:4 *The Message*)

Hot tempers start fights; a calm, cool spirit keeps the peace (Proverbs 15:18 *The Message*)

A man finds joy in giving an apt reply—and how good is a timely word! (Proverbs 15:23)

When my busyness turns my manner brusque and less sensitive, my kids batten down their hearts. Proverbs describes that too: "An offended brother is more unyielding than a fortified city, and disputes are like the barred gates of a citadel" (Proverbs 18:19). Unless I want those painful consequences, I can choose to discipline my children, deal with frustration, express my feelings, and get things done without turbulence. In fact, God promises that my mouth can be a "fountain of life" and my lips can "know what is fitting" (Proverbs 10:11, 32). He tells me that my "cheerful look brings joy to the heart, and good news gives health to the bones" (Proverbs 15:30). Oh, to offer that joy and health to my kids!

Because I want my children to stay open and vulnerable

toward me and my instruction, I have committed myself to shaping a warm, peaceful climate around here. God is helping me, just as He will help you.

Squall-free.

MESSES

I REACHED UNDER THE SINK THIS MORNING TO THROW AWAY a banana peel, but the trash was heaped full, and the plastic bag had scrunched down like a saggy sock. You know, the liner that *should* be folded neatly over the bucket's edges so that old cantaloupe doesn't smear up against the bucket itself. I lifted the bucket out into the middle of the kitchen floor, intending to pull up the sides of the bag. But I had to dig past last night's gravy and a yogurt lid to get at it.

My fumbling set off a chain reaction. Once I moved the yogurt lid, the heaped trash collapsed. A filter full of coffee grounds tumbled onto my foot. Cucumber peels followed, as did a flurry of peanut shells. Not a good start to the day.

Aided by a fistful of paper towels, I wiped everything up, stuffed it all back in that flimsy sack, and hauled the whole mess outside to the garbage can before anything else could spill.

Did I tell you it was 7:00 A.M.? Or that I had on my flannel pajamas with the three-inch red hearts on them—the ones I got last Valentine's Day? Or that my hair had that ratty, smashed-down spot in the back that looks bald from being slept on, even though it really isn't?

It shouldn't have mattered; in five minutes I would have been in the shower.

Instead, I found myself hobbling across the driveway toward the trash can, my arms extended so that the disgusting sack of garbage with sloppy cantaloupe and leftover gravy trickling down the side wouldn't touch my pajamas. A few coffee grounds still clung to my left foot. I had just rounded the corner by the trash cans when a farmer drove up—needing to pick up some papers for a cow being exported to Canada. (He was not in *his* pajamas.)

"Good morning, Cheryl!" What a miserable thing to say. He greeted me as if I always looked fuzzy, faddish, bald. Just an ordinary visit. I was mortified. And his truck cut off my escape.

I mumbled something back and busied myself with the trash until he disappeared into Blake's workroom attached to our garage. Then I hightailed it around his truck and back into the house, hoping for a comforting spell of trauma-induced amnesia.

I expected sympathy from Blake. Instead, he laughed. Laughed, mind you. His wife had been humiliated, and he chuckled. "You've had worse messes, you know."

"Yeah? Like what?" I was itching for a fight, but those pajamas hurt my credibility as an opponent.

"What about the pig fat?

I was down for the count. He had won before I could throw a punch.

He could have reminded me about the time I caught the phone cord on a bowl of zucchini bread batter and dumped it all over the kitchen. And how we found little green strips of zucchini peel in the phone cord, in cabinet hinges, in the refrigerator vent for the next six months.

But no. He had to remind me of how having a pig butchered had prompted me to teach our kids about the olden days, when women cooked with lard. I wanted to show them how those pioneer women melted down that pig fat.

I had put some slabs of fat in shallow pans in the oven and cooked it until it melted. End of lesson. I had no intention of cooking with that body-clogging stuff, so I was going to take it out back and bury it. Unfortunately, it was still hot and liquefied when I began to transport it across some carpeting to the door. You can imagine what happened next. Such a little misstep for such an enormous spill. The pan flew out of my hands as I caught my toe on the carpet's edge. Hot pig fat covered the rug, the wall, the bookcase, the window, and some Fisher-Price Little People lying on the floor.

What a mess. *You* try wiping grease off all that stuff. After futile attempts to swab it up, we called a commercial cleaner.

Unfortunately, he couldn't come until after our dinner party that night.

So we welcomed four couples we didn't know well into our lard-covered home. It certainly was an icebreaker—and a mess by which to gauge all others.

To this day, when we see someone stumbling into horrendous choices with long-term consequences, one of us may say to the other, "She tossed the fat on that one!" or "That's as bad as pig fat!" Translation: some messes just can't be cleaned up overnight.

Good thing God is in the cleanup business. He is a patient soul-janitor who can restore cleanliness and order to lives coated with the grease of bad decisions, the lard of sin. In Ezekiel 36:25–26 and 29, He promises those of us who trust in Him:

> You will be clean; I will cleanse you from all your impurities and from all your idols. I will give you a new heart and put a new spirit in you; I will remove from you your heart of stone and give you a heart of flesh . . . I will save you from all your uncleanness.

Cleaning up sin makes pig fat removal look easy. Jesus knows that it's hard work wiping up the world's biggest mess. After all, He had to die to do it.

MOLEHILLS

"PROBABLY," SAID DALE AT WHATCOM FARMER'S CO-OP, "just one mole is causing the damage in your yard."

Right, I thought. *Looks like an army is tunneling out there and leaving their castings in mounds the size of my three-quart casserole dish.* Not just a couple of piles, either. Those blind, shovel-footed creatures push up soil every few feet. Today before I mowed, I filled a wheelbarrow with molehills.

This is not a new concern. Each year a mole or two scouts out our subterranean landscape and moves in. We know that unless we can catch them, we will be sharing the lawn for months.

Our cat can hear them when they're surfacing. Immobile (but for his quivering chin), he stares at the grass until the eruption begins. When the mole moves out of his tunnel and into the molehill, the cat pounces. End of problem.

I wish it were always that easy. The gardening column in our paper regularly addresses mole control. I have read that some folks try to drive off those diggers by filling their tunnels with dog droppings, odorous plants, whirligig vibrations, firecrackers. Others set traps. But no method *always* works. The Hylers down Axling Road are trying a new tack. A sign in their yard reads: "Free Moles: You Dig."

Me? I just flush them out. I shovel the dirt away from the two-inch hole in the molehill's base, thread a garden hose into the tunnel, and turn on the spigot full blast. The tunnel fills; water burbles from every orifice along the mole's underground route. Usually, he races into a safe corridor in his extensive maze, but every now and then, I will catch him in the dead end of a new tunnel. The water will trap him, forcing him to dig into the light. The second he pops through, I scoop him into my waiting bucket and deport him to the mole colony down by the creek.

Great fun, mole hunts. Those critters are noble adversaries. But when they are undermining my footing, they remind me of uglier realities.

Like jealousy. It can burrow into a life about as fast as a mole digs and can settle into our yearnings for many of the enticements this life offers. You know, into longings for new cars, fine houses, lean bodies, pretty faces, bright brains, attractive personalities, wonderful partners, terrific kids, invigorating jobs, easier lives, good health, white teeth . . . the list is longer than my horse's tail.

Envy burrows into the dark plots of the soul, blindly destabilizing solid spiritual ground. It hurts us individually, and it weakens the body of Christ. "Who can survive the destructiveness of jealousy?" Solomon asks in Proverbs 27:4 (NLT). James explains that "where you have envy and selfish ambition, there you find disorder and every evil practice" (James 3:16).

When jealousy shows up in your mental yard, there is only one thing to do: flush it out. You will be able to spot it, because even if you have tried to keep it underground, it does leave signs—molehills that mar your observable behavior. You may, for example, refuse to celebrate another's job promotion or new home. Maybe you slander or gossip about someone, trying to deflate her standing in a friend's eyes. Or perhaps your simmering jealously has erupted onto something or someone unrelated to the object of your envy. For instance, when feeling covetous, have you ever projected your dissatisfaction onto your children?

As soon as you spot that unspiritual mole, jump on it. Expose it. Call it what it is—wretched jealousy. Admit it to yourself and humbly confess it to God. Take seriously God's warning in Proverbs 14:30: "A heart at peace gives life to the body, but envy rots the bones."

Then dispose of it. Don't allow it to live in you. Refuse to entertain your envious thoughts any longer. Ask God to deport them. Quit wanting what doesn't belong to you and let God's spectacular love for you be enough.

It really is enough. And you don't even have to dig for it.

ROOSTER

THE TEMPERATURE HAD NOT TOPPED FORTY DEGREES ALL day, and an icy drizzle had kept our preschoolers indoors. Their energy was crowding me into corners.

"Shall we go look at the chicks?" I asked. If we drove to the farm store, I knew we would find day-old chicks huddled under the heat lamp out in the store's chilly shed. What perfect entertainment for housebound children. Already, excited yelps hit the ceiling as I dug in the utility room closet for their boots and jackets. We had been planning for our new chickens for weeks, and the kids were ready to bring them home.

Quite a job, choosing chicks. For an hour they waffled, argued, bargained, studied, and finally settled on some of the birds hopping around in the galvanized trough-turned-nursery. An hour later, a peeping box of immature poultry sat in the backseat of the car, with two rapt children buckled in on either side.

Beats me why the decision took so long; young chicks all look alike. Even more bewildering is how anyone can tell newly hatched hens from roosters. I can't, so I don't worry about it. After a few months, all doubts dissipate anyway. Most hens develop a puffy, matronly look, while roosters grow distinctive combs across the tops of their heads, more elaborate plumage, and vicious spurs halfway up their scaly legs; they crow relentlessly.

And some of them get mean. At least our rooster did. He turned from an adolescent—who tagged along with our flock of hens—into a monster. Practically overnight. One morning he blindsided me in the barn as I fed a calf its bottle. Flapping furiously, and aiming his spurs at my bare legs, he flew at me from his perch on the stall as soon as I turned my back to him. I whopped him away with the bottle. He jumped to his feet, shook his feathers, stood on his tiptoes, and crowed. Bottle or no bottle, he had won that encounter and was announcing his lordship of the barn.

"We'll see about that," I said to the strutting bird as I finished feeding the calf.

Within the week, the rooster seized more territory: our backyard. Andrew, age five, had gone out to dig in the garden when the rooster rushed at him from behind the corn. When I heard a racket, I looked out the window. One small boy was charging for the house, screaming, with a rooster in hot pursuit. Andrew didn't wait to hear the bird crow. He headed straight for his arsenal, where he kept an enormous syringe his dad no longer used. He sucked it full of water and headed back outside.

This time, Andrew surprised the rooster. He blasted the bird with water, turned, and ran. The rooster intercepted his route to the door, so the boy streaked for the swing-set, climbed the slide, and wailed. I caught the attacker, threw him back in the barn, and talked Andrew down from the platform.

Blake had come home for lunch when Andrew, his heart set on digging, went back outside. But wouldn't you know it? The rooster had been watching for him from the side of the house. Once Andrew cleared the patio and started across the lawn, the bird flew at him. Andrew dropped his shovel and fled. Never has a boy climbed a slide faster. "Rooooster! Dad! Rooooster!" he howled.

Blake caught that ornery bird mid-crow, clamping his wings to his sides and pointing his feet outward, where he could flail without gouging or bruising anyone. Then, still packing the little tyrant, he walked to the slide. Andrew saw the bird in his arms and shrank to the back of the ledge. "Come down, now, son. He can't get at you anymore," Blake said calmly. Andrew looked doubtful but listened to his dad. With his eye on his feathered adversary, the boy stepped slowly down the ladder.

Then Blake did a curious thing. He knew that roosters, once restrained, aren't really so gutsy. In fact, they can be downright . . . well . . . chicken. So he put the rooster on the ground, positioning him on his side. Next he put his foot over the bird's neck, immobilizing him, before he said, "Now, Andrew. You put your foot here too." Hesitantly, Andrew put his little foot on the rooster's body, next to his dad's. "He won't bother you again," Blake said quietly. With that, Blake picked up the chicken, closed him in a box, and put it in his truck. After lunch, he carted it off to the livestock auction, where someone bought the bird for soup.

That night, as usual, Andrew crawled in Blake's lap with some books, waiting for his dad to read to him. I was washing a skillet in the kitchen, listening with half an ear. "Let's start with this tonight," Blake smiled. He pulled out the Word and opened to Joshua 10. I heard him read about how five Amorite kings had been terrorizing the region; Joshua and his men had captured them and locked them in a cave. Later, Joshua commanded his men to bring them out.

"Listen to this, Cheryl," Blake said, pausing. I dried my hands and leaned against the counter. What I heard next stunned me; it explained why my husband had put his foot on that bird! Here is what he read: "When they had brought these kings to Joshua, he summoned all the men of Israel and said to the army commanders who had come with him, 'Come here and put your feet on the necks of these kings.' So they came forward and placed their feet on their necks. Joshua said to them, 'Do not be afraid; do not be discouraged. Be strong and courageous. This is what the LORD will do to all the enemies you are going to fight'" (Joshua 10:24–25).

I turned back to the sink with tears in my eyes. All these years later, I believe the Holy Spirit must have been whispering in Blake's ear that afternoon. Through that miserable rooster, God had shown Andrew his father's intervention and protection—a foretaste of the way the Lord would intervene for him and protect him all of his life. With God beside him—and inside him—Andrew could have authority over his enemies.

God's foot, Andrew's foot: side by side.

NAME-CALLING

I FIRST MET MANDY AT CHURCH, WHEN MY FAMILY AND I SAT behind her during Sunday morning worship. Our families introduced themselves during the "greeting" part of the service. A few weeks later, I said hello to her as we stood in line at the hardware store. She didn't remember me, but that was understandable; a fifteen-second introduction hardly lands in the brain, much less builds a nest there. We talked for five minutes or so, until the cashier rang up my paintbrushes.

Last night I saw her again, this time at a photography club meeting. Neither of us had seen one another there before, but then, she didn't think she had *ever* seen me before. When I greeted her by name, she looked genuinely baffled. "Do I know you?" she asked.

Happens to me all the time. I have come to accept the fact that I don't make memorable first impressions, and after being a little touchy about it for awhile, I have chosen not to stew over it. But it does bother shy, soft-spoken Kim, who is new in town. "It's like I'm a nonperson," she sighed the other day when I sat beside her at a volleyball game. (Both our daughters were playing.) "I try to meet people, but no one even remembers my name. I'm sick of trying."

Sheepishly, I remembered that I, too, had forgotten her name when we first met. Rarely did I pay fierce attention to names, chalking it up to my distractibility, or poor memory, or busyness.

But when I saw her pain, heard how devalued she felt, I resolved to look at introductions differently. I would pour energy into remembering names. I wanted to be like Doug, whom I had met at a Young Life leaders' gathering my freshman year in college. I had attended with a friend and sat quietly in the group of twenty-five young people. During a break, Doug introduced himself and asked me a few questions about myself. No big deal. I never expected to see him again anyway.

I didn't either—until nearly four years later. I was a college senior and waiting for a friend at the University Center, when Doug walked by. He spotted me out of the corner of his eye. Immediately he burst into an enormous smile, addressed me by my first and last names, and asked me how things were going in my hometown. And he even named the town.

I cannot begin to tell you how I felt. Doug had no self-serving reason to remember me or my name. But he had.

Because God had placed me in his path, he had focused his attention on me. Because Christ had died for me, I had mattered enough to Doug for him to remember my name.

Important things, names. Though I don't like it one bit when a salesperson, in feigned familiarity, keeps repeating my name as he tries to sell me a set of cookware, I warm to the sound of friends greeting me or calling me by name. I feel included. Known. The anonymity and insignificance that can descend on me as I move through crowds vanishes when a friend looks me in the eyes and says my name.

But even when no person remembers who I am, God does. In Isaiah 43, He tells me that He knows me and that even when I feel alone and anonymous, I'm not. He will be paying attention wherever I go. Because of his immeasurable love for me, life won't burn me up or wash me away. Isaiah 43:1–3 explains it:

> But now, this is what the LORD says—
> he who created you . . .
> he who formed you . . .
> "Fear not, for I have redeemed you;
> I have called you *by name*; you are mine.
> When you pass through the waters,
> I will be with you;
> and when you pass through the rivers,
> they will not sweep over you.

When you walk through the fire,
you will not be burned;
the flames will not set you ablaze.
For I am the LORD, your God . . . your Savior.

Maybe Kim will like hearing about Him . . . now that she knows I care enough to remember her name.

AMBUSH

DAN AND JUDY LIVE ON FORTY ACRES UP BURKE ROAD—hilly land with forest, fields, ponds, and plentiful small game. It's coyote territory, and they know it. Over coffee, Dan told us how Duffy, his ten-month-old Labrador–German shepherd cross, had tagged along with him as he augered fence-post holes one Saturday. A hundred yards away, a coyote circled and dodged playfully. When the dog caught sight of him, he stood momentarily frozen as if deciphering the coyote's invitation. Then Duffy lumbered after him. The two disappeared into the woods.

Dan had watched the whole exchange from the back of his tractor. The very second the dog started following the lure, Dan jumped to the ground and ran, shouting, toward the slot in the forest where they had disappeared. As he thundered down the trail, he nearly collided with his pup, who, with ears back and tail tucked, was running for his life, saved by Dan's commotion. A few minutes later, Dan spotted six coyotes trotting from the woods where they had waited for their prey.

We shuddered. When we first came to Goose Ridge, we spotted a pack of fifteen coyotes crossing our bottomland one evening. After that, we kept our cats inside at night and locked up our dogs at bedtime. Then distemper decimated their packs. Their frenetic yips and howls stirred us out of sleep less often. We didn't think about them much anymore, and so let our guard down.

Bad idea. Last week as our dog Iceberg snuffled along the creek bed, we saw the ploy with our own eyes. A large coyote emerged from the undergrowth and tempted our friendly retriever to follow. Bergie dropped to the ground in a crouch. Quick as that, Blake grabbed the shotgun, popped in two shells, and fired into the air. The coyote took off, and Berg ran home. Whew.

Temptations can dress as playful coyotes—alluring to dogs, but deadly, unless the dogs' masters intervene. Decoys call us, too, and we chase them. James explained that each one of us is tempted "when, by his own evil desire, he is dragged away and enticed. Then, after desire has conceived, it gives birth to sin; and sin, when it is full-grown, gives birth to death" (James 1:14–15).

Dogs don't concern themselves with the sin part of it, but

we would be wise to. Temptations come at us from all directions, and their camouflage can confuse us and lead us down paths that can kill us—if not physically, then spiritually or emotionally. Good thing we can turn to our Master . . . Jesus. "Because he himself suffered when he was tempted, he is able to help those who are being tempted" (Hebrews 2:18).

Not only is He *able* to help, but He *will*. Chew on this promise awhile: "And God is faithful; he will not let you be tempted beyond what you can bear. But when you are tempted, he will also provide a way out so that you can stand up under it" (1 Corinthians 10:13). Hear that? He will provide a way out. We can stand up under it.

Tell *that* to the coyotes.

DEEP-BEDDING

IF YOU HAVE EVER WATCHED A COW LIE DOWN, YOU KNOW that she eases to the ground in stages. Usually she'll fold her knees first and slowly sink onto them. Then she'll drop her rump and lower the rest of her massive build. She won't stay in one position for too long, though; more than a few hours on a hard surface can damage muscles and nerves in compressed, heavy tissue, leaving her gimpy—or even paralyzed.

That's why we deep-bed our cows with fir shavings when we ready their winter stalls. Fir (unlike cedar) decomposes well, then disappears when we spread it on our fields later. Until then, that fir provides padding between cows and concrete. They will stay comfortable when the snow flies or when icy rains linger for weeks.

As a newlywed and new "farmer," I misunderstood the concept of deep-bedding. Each day I would head to the barn, take up pitchfork or shovel, and toss all the soiled shavings into the wheelbarrow. It didn't take long to grow a mountain of discarded bedding and to use fresh shavings at a rate that dug into our profits.

Husband Blake clarified the technique. "Don't pitch the whole works, Cheryl. Just scoop the manure off the top and scatter new shavings on top of the old ones."

"But they're soaked!" I protested. (Our cows urinate gallons—and don't discriminate where. Stalls are as good a place as any to let it all go.) "Then their beds only *look* clean. They're rotting underneath!"

Seeing the dismayed look on my face, Blake explained that the urine helped the shavings pack. Excess liquid drained off underneath. Meanwhile, the accumulating bedding protected and cushioned the cows, keeping them warm and comfy. Besides, deep-bedding saved money on shavings. He assured me that every so often we'd scoop the whole mess out with the tractor.

As I was cleaning cupboards this summer, I thought of those stalls—and had to acknowledge that unless I'm vigilant, I make my own deep-beds. When I follow my immediate inclinations, I wrap myself in the insulation of friends, my horse, reading, writing, a long run, or those grocery store brownies (the ones with the thick chocolate frosting). Now those can be good things; my motives aren't all bad. But the sinful part of me wants to bed my personal stall, to insulate myself from the aching for God that, left unattended, can howl from deep inside me.

When I deep-bed myself with those distractions, I am refusing my Papa, who wants me to "seek first his kingdom and his righteousness"; then He will add everything else I need (Matthew 6:33). He asks me to delight myself in Him, and He will give me the desires of my heart (Psalm 37:4). Not just stuff, but the *real* desires.

Please realize that we *all* have mixed motives. We don't usually plan to let those brownies be distractions. Nonetheless, our best intentions can and do easily mutate (just as food or shavings rot) into denial. We ignore our deepest yearnings—which may take a lifetime to satisfy—and pretend we only need something quick and easy. Then we end up distancing ourselves from God. Only after we humble ourselves before Him and remove our distracting idols, can we hear Him speak to us.

As part of the Family Psychology class that I teach, I ask high school seniors to take a twenty-four-hour retreat in solitude. They arrive at Goose Ridge at 6:00 P.M. on a weekend night, and stay until 6:00 the following evening. For that twenty-four hours, they leave distractions behind—no music, computer, junk food, telephone, friends, television, or books (except the Bible). They see and talk to no one. Once they quit anesthetizing their longings with the stuff of daily living, they often feel their hunger for God. When they turn to Him during their retreat time, they are amazed at how He meets them—loving and teaching them throughout their stay.

Have you ever really pitched out your own deep-bedding? Recognized the emotional, intellectual, spiritual, or physical substitutes you stuff yourself with when you are actually hungry for God? Too often, I settle comfortably into my own insulation. Then it's time to haul myself to my feet, locate the pitchfork, and get to work. I don't need to lie in my own rotting, soaked bed—even if it is kinda comfy.

Why should I? The Lord tells me that He "is my shepherd, I shall lack nothing. He makes me lie down in green pastures, he leads me beside quiet waters, he restores my soul" (Psalm 23:1–2 NKJV).

Better than deep-beds any old day.

BLACKBERRIES

MY ARMS AND LEGS ARE COVERED WITH SCRATCHES, MY fingertips with punctures. From the looks of them, you would think I had tangled with a bobcat. I may have preferred that over the thorns. Every fall, despite overalls and long sleeves, I pay a stiff price for my blackberries.

Wild Himalayas. *Rubus procerus.* Warrior vines. They grow in pastures, along fencerows. They compete for sunlight with new forests; they sprout along highways. Their roots spread wide and reach deep—feeding trailers that can grow twenty to thirty feet in a single year, vines that can literally bury a building.

In the early 1980s, old Leroy Wren showed me his family's three-room cabin on Bob Hall Road. A blackberry thicket had wrapped around it for forty years. The day we hacked our way through those brambles, I stepped inside and saw his rusty wringer washer and some tilting bedsprings. But he saw the place as it had been—before the blackberries took over—when he had carried his new bride across the stoop. His babies had been born in that house, eaten soup by the window, peeked over its ledge. "All four of 'em slept in the attic," he laughed. "Me and m'wife slept here." He stubbed the springs with the toe of his boot. He walked to the sink and looked down. "We was watched over, I tell ya. The Good Lord protected us." Seasons skipped across his cloudy eyes. He had lived there during the lean years of the 1930s, when the barn burned and he lost three fingers at the mill. But God's thorny protection had guarded his joy—kept that fruit intact.

When World War II broke the Depression's stranglehold, he moved his clan to bigger lodgings a half mile north—and gave the cabin to the blackberries.

Vines own part of our creek, and that's where I pick. They grow with fantastic vigor and produce huge, sweet, nourishing berries. Clusters hang heavy with abundant fruit. In just a few hours, I load my buckets and bring home enough for a year's worth of pies and fruit smoothies. I can't begin to harvest them all. Leftovers turn the ground purple with their juice for weeks.

But only when I am armed with lop shears—and expecting injury—do I risk picking. Berries, you see, develop on the previous year's growth. As new vines mound and crosshatch over them, they form an umbrella of protection over the berries that deters many birds and animals—as well as humans. Given that barrier of thorns, the berries can usually ripen without being plucked, hidden safe inside the mound.

Someday, I thought as I battled this summer's vines, *I'll get this. I'll grasp God's instruction hidden in these strange plants.*

Then I thought of Leroy. Just as thorny vines guard berries, the Lord held his protective umbrella over the Wrens. No, He didn't deflect all pain away from the family in that cabin, but He brought them through some ugly years. Their joy grew and ripened. He was guarding them, all right, and they knew it.

Leroy might use other words, but today I bet he would say something like this to God:

> Therefore let everyone who is godly pray to you
> while you may be found;
> surely when the mighty waters rise,
> they will not reach him.
> You are my hiding place;
> you will protect me from trouble
> and surround me with songs of deliverance. (Psalm 32:6–7)

Amen to that.

Blackberry pie, anyone?

FERTILIZER

WITH APRIL'S WARMER DAYS, THE FIRST CUTTING HAS begun its explosive rush to the sky. Timothy, orchard, and rye grasses erupt like verdant lava—in a green so intense, I have to look away to the garden soil or the pond, resting my eyes before they hungrily swallow more. But by May, the farmers will take it all down. Tractors will pull dinosaur-necked "green choppers" across their cropland, pulverizing the grass before they load it into silos as winter fodder for the county's dairy cows.

Once the choppers carve their stubble stripes, the manure spreading begins. Enormous sprinkler "guns" spray the brown gunk on larger fields in the valley below. But our hilly ridge calls for manure trucks. Like carrion beetles, those trucks fill up on the waste from raised lagoons or from pits beneath the cow barns. At the field's edge, the driver pauses, reads the lay of the land, and revs the engine. Then he opens the spigot at the rear of the tank and, like a giant beast, the truck empties its bowels on the newly mown field.

Cow manure stinks. It puddles. It coats everything it lands on. The whole process is so disgusting that when we moved here twenty some years ago, I couldn't believe it actually happened. "How can anyone live through this?" I would groan. "What? They do it three times a year?"

Maybe the odor killed some of my nasal receptors, or maybe I just got used to it, but eventually I settled down. Believe it or not, I now consider manuring one more step in life's rhythm around here, a necessary component of crop growth. Do you know why? After its initial assault, manure soaks in or dries. The smell subsides in a day or two. Then it begins its wonderful work. It feeds the grass, and that fresh greenery jumps up all over again, fragrant and punctuated with dandelions. When the grass dances with a late afternoon westerly, I thank the Lord for manure.

Several years back, I met an old schoolmate in the grocery's bread aisle. There, from her strapped-in perch on a motorized shopping cart, she told me how she had been caught under the nozzle and coated with manure. No, not the cow variety, but the life-event sort. You know, the situational manure that transforms life's lovely landscape into a putrid, smelly scene. For months, that young mother had visited doctors, trying to ferret out the cause of back and leg pain.

Sciatica? Arthritis? Finally, when she went blind in one eye, the doctors keyed in on the cause: multiple sclerosis.

Her world tumbled. Grim reports of the disease's potential progression left her depressed. She feared for the stability of their two preschool daughters. Meanwhile, the prospects of his wife's shortened life in a wheelchair shook her husband's commitment to their marriage. *Where was God in this, anyway?* she had wondered.

As time crept on, the Lord answered her question. No, He didn't stop the disease's ravages. Yes, her daughters grew clingy as their mom grew sicker. And yes, her husband grappled unsteadily with their relationship as his vigorous, youthful wife's body aged and twisted before his eyes.

But greenery grew inside her that had lain dormant before she was doused with MS. I listened with something akin to reverence as she told me, "If I could choose between my pre- and post-MS lives, I'd keep the disease, even with the emotional and physical pain it has caused. Because now," and she paused a moment, "because now I *know* God will keep my soul intact. I am no longer afraid of anything." She said the word *know* with a quiet conviction that quaked the earth beneath me.

Her "knowing" wasn't just an opinion, an intellectual exercise. She had experienced God, felt Him closer to her than her own skin. She *knew* that God would never leave her nor forsake her (Hebrews 13:5). She saw firsthand that "in all things

God works for the good" (Romans 8:28). After all, she loved Him, and He loved her. And so she didn't fear for herself or her daughters or her husband. God's perfect love had truly cast out her fear. Whether He repaired her in this life or the next, she knew that everything would ultimately be all right.

I hugged her as we said good-bye, and I watched the back of her head as her cart hummed away, hauling her collapsed body toward the checkout stand. In that moment, I imagined the prevailing westerly brushing a grass sea, and I saw her healed, waltzing with God.

And once again, I thanked Him for manure.

DROOPY

I washed the windows less than two weeks ago, but muddy cat prints already smear seven of the panes, thanks to Droopy. Whenever that cat wants to come inside, he jumps up on an outside ledge and peers into the house until he spots me. Then he goes to the window nearest my location, stands on his hind legs, and drags his claws across the window in a raspy screech. His technique is flawless; I let him in immediately.

Do I have a choice? Not if I want to stay home—or avoid earplugs. I have tried ignoring him, dropping the blinds, or going to a different room, but he outlasts me. Sooner or later, the scratching wears me down, and I relent.

I wouldn't mind so much if after I opened the door he would crunch a few tasty kiblets, jump in the chair, and nap awhile, but that rarely happens. Droopy, you see, cannot make up his mind. Within minutes of his entry, he is back at the door, yowling to go outside. Not scratching; scratching gets him *into* the house. Yowling gets him *out*. He knows that I—motivated by an aversion to cleaning cat mess off carpets—will *not* ignore him when he whines.

Too bad, really, that I like the cat so much. Otherwise, I would find him some owners he couldn't train. When I brought him home as a kitten, I had no idea he would require so much maintenance. But I have resigned myself to the fact that this cat vacillates. One minute he wants to hunt mice, the next he longs to come inside and sit in my lap, drooling as I pet him. In and out, in and out, in and out: he repeats the cycle a dozen times a day.

I had let Droopy into the house for the fourth time this morning when I opened the Word to the book of James. That disciple had watched people vacillate between following God and following their own selfish inclinations. He had seen how a person would ask God for wisdom, then question that wisdom. In response, James wrote, "But when he asks [for wisdom], he must believe and not doubt, because he who doubts is like a wave of the sea, blown and tossed by the wind . . . he is a double-minded man, unstable in all he does" (James 1:6, 8).

When I recognized myself in James' words, I thought about buying myself a flea collar. Maybe I *should* dress like Droopy. Might as well; I can certainly waver like he does. How eagerly I copy that cat when I run into the safe, warm house of God's affectionate love, then turn right around and dash outside to chase down rodents of approval from people I want to please. I hunt for praise, swallow it, then hurry home to God when my stomach starts churning from all that conditional acceptance.

Too often, I seek God's guidance, find it in the Word, then instead do exactly as my pride or insecurity dictates. When consequences crop up, I'm back at God's door, scratching.

Just like the cat is now. Hold on, Droopy, I'm coming.

NORTHEASTER

THE DAY THE TEMPERATURE DROPPED, RAIN HAD BEEN PELT-ing us for weeks. Everywhere, ditches spilled their banks, flooding fields. Rivers threatened their dikes. Even here in the hills, the soil was completely saturated; I splashed wherever I walked.

Then, like a freight train changing direction, the air began a slow shift. In the space of an hour, the southwest winds that had been delivering our ocean-spawned winter downpour quit. The rain slowed to a sprinkle. The air grew still, as if holding its breath.

So gently, a wispy breeze out of the northeast puffed in. For a half an hour, snow filtered down, lightly layering the sodden earth. Then it, too, stopped. The breeze swept the murky clouds back to sea and scoured the sky. Sunshine and color washed the landscape. I ran outside with my camera.

I didn't stay long. The new wind, stronger now, was shooting down the Fraser River canyon, carting air straight off the Canadian prairie. It was cold. When I checked the thermometer hanging outside, the temperature had dropped to twenty degrees and was still falling. Looked like a stiff northeaster was moving in.

No problem. We made it a habit to be prepared for storms. We had plenty of groceries. Three cords of firewood waited in the lean-to. Jugs of water sat in the storage room. Blake would come home from his veterinary calls soon, and we would eat hot soup and bread as the storm blew itself out.

Unknown to me, radio airwaves were warning residents to take cover. Forecasters predicted dangerous windchill readings: temperatures below ten degrees Fahrenheit and hurricane-force winds. They were right.

At fifty miles per hour, wind moans in old firs. When it hits seventy-five, the sound changes to a high-pitched keening. But when wind gusts to one hundred miles per hour, it screams in the trees like a wild animal. We had never heard or seen anything like it.

Over the next three days, groves of hundred-year-old trees fell, the soggy soil surrendering their roots to the frigid wind. Power lines collapsed with them, disabling water and heat supplies. Icy roads and flying debris made travel risky. Livestock suffered miserably.

Including ours. After dark, the second night of the storm, Blake burst into our unlit house. A fallen cedar tree had knocked out our power, and we had no generator. Though the fire kept us comfortable, we depended upon our electric pump to draw water for our livestock.

I heard my husband's muffled voice from the closet, where he was donning extra layers of clothing. "The cows are out of water. We have to haul it."

"How?" I asked. "The pump's out."

"We'll open the well. C'mon." With that, he pulled on his woolen facemask and disappeared out the door.

I quickly bundled up and followed him, deeply concerned. Without water, our cows would dehydrate fast in that wind and wouldn't digest their alfalfa efficiently. If they couldn't process their feed, they wouldn't stay warm.

Once outside, I shrank from the blast. Blake had already loaded every bucket we owned into the back of the pickup. I climbed in the truck, and we drove through the field to the well—a three-foot-wide hole in the ground. Blake wrested the concrete lid to one side, clumsily tied a rope to a five-gallon bucket, dropped it into the opening, and started pulling up water.

In that gale, everything took longer. Though the moaning wind and bellowing heifers urged us on, the cold numbed our fingers and slowed our limbs. We had to crouch against the wind or we would topple over. Tediously, we raised bucket after bucket, pouring the precious liquid into the waiting containers.

But the wind and cold tackled us, thwarted us. Buckets

sloshed when we pulled them out of the well, coating the ground along its edge with a thick layer of ice and making it a treacherous place to stand; one slip and we would tumble into the hole. The wind blew the water sideways as we poured it, icing the truck with every splash. As we drove over the frozen, bumpy field, more water slopped out, freezing instantly.

By the time we reached the trough, the buckets were only half-full. Ice covered the truck bed, making it nearly impossible to stand up in it, much less carry a bucket across it. I fell twice, spilling even more. All the while, the cows lowed mournfully, sucking down the water as fast as we could deliver it. We made several trips before they seemed satisfied.

My shoulders were aching, my hands numb when Blake spotted the heifer off by herself. Though she wasn't due to calve for another week, two hooves protruded from under her tail, a common sign of an impending delivery. "If that calf stays out here, it'll be dead in minutes," Blake said. Earlier that day, a farmer had found a baby bull frozen before he ever learned to stand, a victim of windchill.

I have tagged along with Blake for a lot of calvings, so I wasn't surprised when he grabbed those tiny feet, and pulled until the calf slid out of her mother; nothing unusual there. But this time, he didn't even let the calf hit the ground. He caught the newborn in his arms, and we ran for the truck. When I opened the door, he heaved the slimy calf onto the bench seat and started the engine. She flopped there, limp. I stuck a piece of straw in her nose to tickle her into breathing, and we bumped across the field toward home.

Lots of northeasters have blown through Goose Ridge in years since, but none have affected me like that one did. Smack in the middle of that terrifying storm, God reigned. When wind and ice could have sent one of us tumbling into the depths of that well, He guarded us. When animals that depended upon us needed water, He gave us a way to provide it. And when that deadly storm wanted to suck the life out of everything, He brought new life into the middle of it—a calf who later stood on wobbly legs in a corner of our garage.

> Praise the LORD from the earth,
>   you great sea creatures and all ocean depths,
> lightning and hail, snow and clouds,
>   stormy winds that do his bidding,
> you mountains and all hills,
>   fruit trees and all cedars,
> wild animals and all cattle,
>   small creatures and flying birds . . .
>   Let them praise the name of the LORD. (Psalm 148:7–10, 13)

Not all storms blow out of the northeast, you know. Life storms can blast in from any direction, often without warning. But even in their midst, we can praise our Creator, to whom all storms must answer.

PRAYER BALES

OVER AT WESTLYN FEED, PETE STEIGER SHOWED ME A HAY
sample. "I've moved a lot of this," he said, as he yanked a bale
off a fragrant stack. "Clean, local, third cutting. Few stems.
Leafy. Good protein. Your horse won't waste much of it."
Pete has sold us hay for years. If he says it's good quality, I
believe him. I ordered 150 bales.

The next day he delivered it—the difficult part of his job.
For small orders in little barns like ours, Pete stows the hay
alone, and by hand. His only tools are hay hooks (which look
like huge fishhooks with handles) and heavy gloves. After he
backed his truck around to the gate, he began the strenuous
work of stacking those sixty-pounders.

He moved them one at a time. With his hooks securely
planted in each end, he hoisted every bale up and into the pile.
Again and again he wedged those loaves of grass into a tight,

crisscross pattern. Up one side, he built a hay staircase of sorts, so I could get to the top of the sturdy structure.

When he finished unloading, I paid him and watched his truck lumber away. Then I climbed the stack, cut the twine binding a new bale, and tossed two flakes down to my horse. After dinner I'd return again and throw him two more. He was munching peacefully as I headed for the house, where I kicked off my boots, plucked hay from my sweater, washed my hands, and curled up on the couch to read the Word and write in my journal.

After praying that God would direct me, I started thumbing through Scripture's pages, with no particular destination in mind. Then my eyes lit on the conversation between Jesus and Peter in the gospel of John, where Jesus tells that disciple, "Feed my lambs . . . take care of my sheep" (John 21:15–16). My attention riveted on those words as I thought about God's terrific timing. It was no coincidence that He spoke to me in those terms, through that very passage. He knew that I had just fed newly stacked, sweet hay to my horse, a task that would help me picture my responsibility to feed His children—especially the young people in my life.

I read the passage twice, then sat still for a long time, while hay bales and lambs and horses and children found their places in my thoughts. Then this prayer took shape on the journal page in front of me.

Lord, I do care about feeding Your lambs, especially the children You have entrusted to me. Please stack Your good feed in me, so that I have a barn full of nourishment to dispense. As I love and teach Your children, will You fill me with bales of wisdom to

- ❧ *Encourage tenderness*
- ❧ *Balance justice and mercy*
- ❧ *Seek truth*
- ❧ *Listen well*
- ❧ *Be flexible*
- ❧ *Refuse temptation*
- ❧ *Discipline consistently*
- ❧ *Protect appropriately*
- ❧ *Love deeply*
- ❧ *Laugh often*

Only You can stow that kind of fodder in me. I thank You even as I wait.

In Jesus' name, amen.

In the intervening years, God has loaded my soul-barn—as I have studied His Word, prayed, and learned through circumstances and relationships. Meanwhile, He has fed me His help and direction as I have needed it. High protein. No stems. Absolutely no waste, either.

SURROGATE

I FOUND THE BURROW IN THE WOODSHED AROUND DINNER-
time. At eight cubic feet, it was nearly large enough for a
retriever and her pups, but Rookie wanted it bigger. The dog
was digging urgently, in a staccato, paddling motion, the dirt
flying out of the hole behind her. She was panting hard.

"Here, Rook . . . here, girl," I called. She lifted her head out
of the hole, a glazed expression in her eyes. I grabbed her collar and pulled her toward me, then led her to the house,
where her whelping box waited. Even as we walked, her back
humped up for another contraction. Those pups would arrive
soon. Her compact belly told us to expect a small litter, maybe
three or four pups—a good size for a first-time mother.

A few days earlier, I had hauled home a refrigerator box,
laid it on its side, and lined it with blankets, making a dog cave
to rival any she would dig. Now I led Rookie to the box's open

end. Before she started laboring, she had crawled inside with me a couple of times, so she already knew the territory.

This time, though, she climbed in by herself, scraped the blankets into a lumpy mat, and lay down. A single pup arrived within twenty minutes. Though we waited for hours, none followed. A thorough exam and an oxytocin injection (to contract her uterus) told us that she had finished birthing. She'd grown one pup, and that was all.

Over the next week Rookie mothered well, and her baby grew fat. I was thinking that we would all breeze through this puppy business, when the phone rang. Johanne, a friend who lives two hours south of us, called to say her retriever had undergone an emergency cesarean section, yielding ten pups. The mother was struggling. After the trauma of surgery, she didn't have enough milk. Would we consider putting five of the babies with Rookie?

When Johanne came in with the puppies, we took Rookie's plump, sleepy baby away from her side and rubbed him over each of the newborns, to give them his scent. Then we snuggled each one up to a teat for a belly-filling meal. From that moment on, Rookie adopted those pups. As her milk filled them, its familiar scent also passed from Rookie to the babies, strengthening their bond. They settled into the box contentedly.

Three days later, we got another call. My sister's collie had recently delivered twelve pups. That mother had developed severe mastitis (a mammary infection). Fever had disabled her and dried up much of her milk. Though she could probably feed half of her babies, she couldn't manage all of them. Could we take six pups?

I wavered. Rookie already had six pups, plenty for a new mother. How would she handle twelve? We decided to give it a try. If we could just grant the mother collie a few days' respite, her milk supply would recover, and her babies could return home.

When the new batch of puppies arrived, Rookie looked bewildered. These mottled pups bore no resemblance to her golden babies. With their long noses, the collies looked more like possums than dogs. Unlike the sleepy little retrievers, these creatures acted like raccoons, frantically nuzzling, clawing, yipping.

But they needed Rookie—and she sensed it. Within minutes of their arrival, she adopted the whole lot of them. As twelve assorted pups crowded along her underside and nursed, Rookie sniffed them all, then lay back and sighed.

The evening after the collies showed up, the kids and I were reading on the sofa. We had already plowed through two library books when I opened the Word to Ephesians 1. There I read about how God lovingly chose us to be adopted into His family through Jesus—and how happy He is to forgive us. I was going to read more, when seven-year-old Andrew stopped me. "Kinda like Rookie and the pups," he said.

"What?" I asked.

"Adopted. Like Rookie adopted the pups. She made them her very own."

"Yep," I nodded. "Kinda like Rookie and the pups."

CATERPILLARS

TENT CATERPILLARS INFESTED OUR TREES THE YEAR ANDREW learned to read. Each year we had a few, but this spring, the old cut-leaf birch housed at least ten of the foot-long webs, while the smaller fruit trees held three or four each. Their webs resembled layers of fiberglass angel hair and sheltered thousands of the tiny striped caterpillars.

Avery thought they were wonderful. When she saw them marching in a line out of their gauzy nests toward the leaves they would devour en masse, she came in the house, shouting, "Momma, they're walking in little lines! They're fuzzy, and have blue spots on 'em. Do they bite?"

Though I didn't share her enthusiasm as I watched them defoliate my trees, I assured her that they were perfectly harmless to little girls. "Well, can I play wif 'em?" she begged.

I couldn't see why not, so I reached in the cupboard and

pulled down the jar we saved for such occasions—the one with the holes punched in the lid. I handed it to her, and she sprinted out the door.

For the next month, the caterpillars lived with us. Avery carried them in the basket on her bike, put them in her pockets, and filled jars and Cool Whip containers with them, along with whatever leaves they were destroying that day. And she named them. Since she couldn't write yet, she recruited her first-grade brother who, she reasoned, could print *anything*. Before long, every container had a list taped to its side, identifying the occupants as Lucy, Hank, Sheri, Steve, Bob, Doris, Gail, Kent. I wondered how our friends would feel about having caterpillars as namesakes.

Within a few weeks, the inch-long insects Avery had been gathering grew. Now three inches and voracious, they traveled faster and farther, and squirmed harder when she picked them off a branch. I was ready for them to pupate.

One night Avery had a herd of about thirty of them spread out on the covers of her bed. Part of the evening ritual now included tucking her in and saying goodnight to all her caterpillars. After we prayed, I kissed her on the forehead. (I refused to kiss the caterpillars.) I helped her put them back in the jar, set it on the bedside table, and turned out the light.

Whether she removed the lid for one last peek before she fell asleep, or whether I didn't close the lid tightly enough, I'll never know. But in the morning, only leaves remained in the jar. The caterpillars were gone.

Avery was inconsolable. It made no difference to her that ten thousand more waited for her out in the orchard. These were her friends! They had names, and they were missing!

"I'll bet they're playing hide-and-seek, Avery," I suggested.

She sniffled. "Tink so?"

"Let's look." We found about half of them. They were traversing the bed frame and the lampshade, crawling up a stuffed bear and into a shoe. Three were traveling in a line across the window frame—the closest thing in the room to a tree branch. I wondered where the others had climbed—until Avery told me: "Prob'ly the rest of 'em went outside to play, huh, Momma? I'll go find 'em." With that, she skipped away. I heard the front door slam.

Over time, I have come to see those runaway caterpillars as symbolic of the challenging character issues children—and their parents—can face. Those voracious insects of impatience, selfishness, insensitivity, and negativity can defoliate our lives if they crawl around unapprehended. But as we learn to "take captive every thought to make it obedient to Christ" (2 Corinthians 10:5), the Holy Spirit will wrap our thoughts in Wisdom's silk and transform those traits into "love, joy, peace, patience, kindness, goodness, faithfulness, gentleness and self-control" (Galatians 5:22).

Good names for caterpillars.

PAUSING

WHILE PROWLING THE RACKS AT THE CARD SHOP THE OTHER day, I found a timely birthday greeting. On the front was a black-and-white photo of a bespectacled grandma, her eyebrows raised all-knowingly. Underneath it, a caption read, "Some things are more difficult than being a year older, dearie." Inside the card, the punch line read, "You could be a week late."

I bought it on the spot . . . but not because I worried about another mouth to feed. At my yearly checkup, the doctor had asked about my cycles. You know, the monthly ones that prompt gynecologists to ask nosy questions.

"A week late last month," I replied. "Peculiar, huh?"

"About time," she said. "You *are* pushing 50."

As if I didn't know that. I can handle the half-century comments from my kids, but her words bothered me. I felt like the fruitful, youngish woman in me had run out, slammed the screen door, and skedaddled to the back side of the hill. Where things wrinkle. And dry up. And quit.

Ornery doctor. She must have skipped breakfast, to be making such nasty comments. I put them out of my mind.

But when I got home, our twelve-year-old retriever struggled to her feet to greet me. Her teeth are worn to the gums; she sleeps long and snores loudly. What's more, our cat Molly—at nearly fourteen—couldn't leap onto the bed. She climbed it, because she's stiff, weakening in her years. Then my husband came in, graying, with deep creases around his eyes. Why had I not noticed all this before?

To top it all off, the late October leaves were shriveling, the grass browning. All the magical birds—swallows, geese, songbirds—had flown to warmer climes. We were left with raucous crows, gulls, starlings. Daylight was failing a little more each day. Everywhere I looked, life was descending into death.

I didn't fix a very good dinner that night.

Later, I walked out to the barn, where my horse was munching his evening hay. By the way, he's twenty-two now, and semiretired, with white hairs peppering his mane and face. I ran my hand down his lovely old neck and cried. I felt the pain of this fallen world, my dying self, my dying life.

I like my life, and I don't want to lose it. The years the locust ate when I was a child have been restored to me, for the time being. And I would like them to endure. I don't want to grow old and sick—and then die. I want to wrap myself in the people (my husband, kids, family, friends, students) and things that I enjoy and have them last forever.

The impatient, faithless, immediate part of me wants to create my own heaven—my own perfect garden. After all, the real heaven I have heard about lurks out of reach, vague and hazy. How can I think about someplace I am *told* I will like when so many great things surround me—and I am so busy trying to hang on to them?

But they slip away, even as I grasp at them. Neither seasons nor my aging cat should tighten my grip on what I have right now, but instead ought to point toward what's to come, toward heaven.

According to our pastor, when God says in Revelation 21:5, "I am making everything *new*," He uses a Greek word for *new* that means *restored*. Think of that when you read the following: "Then I saw a new heaven and a new earth, for the first heaven and the first earth had passed away" (Revelation 21:1). That means that wherever things are ruined, diseased, or overcrowded, they will be remade . . . like new! Contaminated landfills? Squalid slums? Exhausted farmland? Won't find 'em there.

Even better, as 1 John 3:2 tells us, "We know that when he appears, we shall be like him, for we shall see him as he is." Emotional distance? Cruelty? Rejection? Misunderstanding?

Nowhere! We will bask in absolute tenderness with God—and each other.

One afternoon when our son was five, I was telling him about heaven and reading him descriptions from the Word. His response is etched in my memory. "Oh, Momma, don't you just want to go there? Won't it be *wunnerful?*" He was jumping and spinning around me with his arms outspread, as if he could already see it, feel it, hear it. And the ecstasy of it all whirled him around the room.

I try to do that now, to take God at his Word so completely that I feel like whirling. Doing so gives me courage to acknowledge the ache in living. Nowadays, when life stabs at me, I can look past the sadness toward heaven. I like to think of 2 Corinthians 4:17–18: "For our light and momentary troubles are achieving for us an eternal glory that far outweighs them all. So we fix our eyes not on what is seen, but on what is unseen. For what is seen is temporary, but what is unseen is eternal."

Glory. Where we will never grow old—and nothing, nothing, nothing will ever go wrong again.

CONCLUSION

A CRESCENT MOON SKIPS, FLIMSY, ACROSS THE NIGHT SKY. Like a clipped fingernail, it eventually drops like debris into the inattentive horizon. Unless sunset or stars dress it up, it's not much of a show.

But for the moon's full phase, I order front-row seats. When it comes on stage through a cleft in the mountains, even my son plops in a chair to watch. One fall night it rose costumed as a can of paint—with the lid pried off. We were looking straight into its glowing, milky contents. Within minutes, an experienced hand brushed its color over everything: pond water, aspen leaves, sleeping cattle, our bare feet and jeans.

"Is that just moonlight?" Andrew asked. He was fourteen, so the night sky shouldn't have surprised him. I looked again. Was he seeing something I didn't? I paused, and saw more deeply.

"Just moonlight." I replied. The higher the moon rose, the more its paint saturated the landscape. Blades of grass lit up. Ancient firs gleamed. Andrew's face looked radiant, illumined with moon paint. Everything glowed bright, tender.

Was this my son? Were those our dogs sleeping in the grass? Was this Goose Ridge? Nothing looked the same. In a few brief moments, the world as I knew it had transformed into something recognizable but new—its flaws smoothed, its predictable features redrawn.

Sometimes I think that the kingdom of God is like moon-paint, which its Painter brushes backwards through time and memories in a kind of retrospective redemption. As we who love Christ move toward heaven, isn't it possible that the edges of God's kingdom can brush not only the present, but our personal histories as well—transforming our naiveté, or pain, or pessimism with the light of His presence?

I think so. Holy paint not only colors my life today, but it has also redecorated my memories with a more forgiving, tender tint, a deeper-hued understanding—and a brighter, more hopeful aspect. It has shaped my view from Goose Ridge—and I am grateful.

Who paints like that, anyway?

Only Jesus.